To Ouanae,
may this b[e]
be a bless[ing in]
your life!

[signature] 3/19/11

To ammar,

man this book is

be a blessing

your life

[signature] 3/9/11

WITHOUT PERMISSION

A Spiritual Journey to Healing

Sharon R. Wells

TESTIMONIALS

There are many topics still viewed as taboo in the church. Sexual abuse is one of them. Sharon R. Wells brings much needed light to this subject as she courageously explores her own battle with this issue. Sharon's transparency with this remarkable piece of literary genius will no doubt inspire, encourage, and uplift those struggling with their own demons while opening dialogue on a subject that needs to be addressed in the kingdom. Kudos to Sharon R. Wells on her new book, "Without Permission." Job well done!

— Evangelist Cheryl Lacey Donovon

Finally, a book that unveils the shame and secrecy of sexual molestation, without artificial fanfare or added puffery of abuse that leaves many victims; victimized! Without Permission is an enlightening account of victim, to survivor, to thriver! This no holds barred journey is a welcome asset to sexual abuse survivors, organizations, churches and book clubs throughout the world! Whether you've been abused or know someone who has been, this book is relevant and timely for all! Thank you Sharon for sharing your story!

— Cherilyn Vonn, Author, Sexual Abuse Activist,
Speaker, Radio/TV Personality

Published by:
Angel Wings Publications, LLC
P.O. Box 96
Vauxhall, NJ 07088
www.angelwingspublications.com
angelwingspub@yahoo.com

Library of Congress Cataloging–in-Publication Data:
Wells, Sharon R, 2011
Without Permission/Sharon R. Wells
1st ed. p. cm.
ISBN: 978-0-615-23142-6
First Printing, 2011
Printed in the United States of America

To my daughters and granddaughters,
Shahnta, Amber, Sanai and Khyla,
Thank you for enriching my life!

To my mother, thank you for being my rock!

To Rhonda, you're the best sister in the world!

To my family, I love you all!

To every person, whose life has been affected by abuse, I
pray that your spirit will heal and fly freely.

In memory of my loved ones:

Idella Woods (1902-1990)
Nathaniel Malone, Sr. (1919-2005)

HONORARY MENTION

A book of this nature would not be possible without the creative assistance and support of those that helped push me toward fulfillment of my dream. Special thanks are given to the following individuals:

Book Cover Design: Stephen Swinton – Swinton Studio

Editors: Anita Levine and Lorraine Elzia

Photos: Mark Anthony – PortraitEFX of Middlesex

Website designer for Without Permission: Jeff McCollum

Transcriber for the personal stories and true to life accounts: Eileen Knoud

Interior Book Design: Jessica Tilles of TWA Solutions & Services

Book Contributors: DeShannon Bowens, Stephen L. Braveman, M.A., L.M.F.T., D.S.T., Nanette M. Buchanan, Cheryl Lacey Donovon, Pastor Cynthia Dunbar, Carol A. Ennis, Nickolas J. McDaniel, Cherilyn Vonn, Nan Wise, LCSW, ACSW, BCD

A special thank you to those who had the perseverance to stand behind me and believed in me against all odds: DeShannon Bowens, Seth Daniels, Elissa Gabrielle, Grace Gordon, Dee Jackson Field, Armanda L. Freeman, Cari Jackson, Stephanie L. Jones, Myrna Lyle, Trena Mann Araujo, Tanya Newkirk, Lizette Pabellon, Lenora R. Robinson, Linda Wickliffe-Farid.

Extended heart-filled shows of love and thanks to all those that touched my life and helped me grow whose names are not mentioned above. Your placement in my life has been a gift from God, and you know your importance, even if I have failed to say it or mention you by name. Please blame it on my head and not my heart. There is no way I can ever give full recognition to all who have touched my life or helped me make my dreams a reality, but to all the silent soldiers who went to war with me in this battle, to you, my fearless angels along this mission, I say thank you.

ACKNOWLEDGEMENTS

In order to take flight, there must be wind underneath the wings. I am grateful to others for helping my message fly on the supportive shoulders of a wing and a prayer. This book is possible because I have been blessed with a flock of Angels too massive to name individually. So, instead I give you all collective praise.

When I was weak and didn't think I had the strength to tell my story, thank you, my Angels, which reminded me that strength is a state of mind, and I had the power to overcome any obstacle along my path.

When I was filled with self-doubt, uncertain which way to turn, thank you, my Angels that helped me find my way by reminding me that my current location did not have to be my destination.

When I felt unworthy of being a poster child for a cause, thank you, my Angels that reminded me that to whom much is given, much is required and that God supplies the tools needed for those whom He calls.

When I needed support you gave it, when I needed direction you provided it, when I needed love or just a friend, you were there. You know who you are; and my Angels…I thank you.

I never would have been able to fly this journey alone, and I thank each of you for being the wind beneath me when I needed it, and for being my Angel Wings.

~ Sharon R. Wells

FOREWORD
~ Pastor Cynthia J. Dunbar

I can recall sitting in the office with Ms. Wells as the masks were removed and the past was in our faces; sharing, laughing and almost near tears, realizing how so many little girls—now grown up women—have suffered the ugly painful sin of incest and sexual abuse, and yes, without permission.

As you, the reader, begin to embrace this book, I trust that you will understand the need for the writer being so candid, as she reveals the little secrets that almost destroyed the beauty that she now sees. Incest and sexual abuse are dirty little secrets that few care to touch, because it involves so many people. I am sure that you will be blessed, if you open your hearts and accept the angel who God has used to help those who may continue to suffer because their voices can't be heard. Sharon R. Wells felt the pain and destruction of sexual abuse; now with joy and excitement we celebrate her joys, and victories for not allowing her past to depict her future.

I am thrilled to see that this young woman has picked up the mantle to educate people of all races and colors to show how the secret of sexual abuse can destroy you, if you allow it to.

Pastor Cynthia J. Dunbar
My Sister My Friend Ministries

TABLE OF CONTENTS

Part III: Taking Back Your Power

Monsters can only live in the dark; bringing their horrors to light strips them of their tormenting power, making them weak while giving the victim strength. Sexual abuse is an everyday occurrence perpetrated by individuals from all walks of life. I have chosen to withhold the names and identities of my abusers. This decision is based on my desire to respect the relationships of the people I love and whose lives would be negatively impacted if names were revealed. Finding a way to transform from a victim to victor and reach empowerment beyond abuse is the message; revelation of my perpetrator's identities is irrelevant. The most valuable benefits received along this journey have been learning how to heal, forgive and love myself; those are the blessings of wisdom that I wish to pass along to others.

Without Permission

My world of innocence, my world of purity, sanity and
bliss was changed the moment you touched me,
forced me, demanded we kiss.
Each time I cried, slowly died. I even asked why
you said you loved me. I learned later that love never lies.

My world of comfort, my world of peace
was distorted, contorted, fulfilling your daily needs.
Without permission, you continued to proceed.

My world filled with lace and crimson, dolls, and fairytales was
a facade, an illusion, a storybook of dreams. How real it
seemed I was loved by my family, surrounded by blessings, but
it was you who embraced me with undesired caressing.

I never said yes, I was too scared to say no.
I wanted it to stop. I didn't know who to tell, or where to go.
You touched me, made me feel dirty, and then...
You'd talk and play with me, as though we were friends.

I told my mother, I couldn't bear the thought of my sin.
I couldn't bear the thought of you touching me again.
Without permission, you invaded my body, my mind, my world,
you ruined my childhood, the innocence of a little girl.

I grew up with the memories, the tears and the pain,
I had nightmares, blamed myself, struggled with
early romances, true love is not the same.
Without permission, you've become a constant in my life,
I now speak out for girls, mothers and wives.

Those who find themselves struggling as the result of abuse,
those who want to give in because without permission they've been used.

Nanette M. Buchanan
© 2010

Introduction

*"Angels are real spiritual beings documented throughout the
bible. They assume different forms and possess a wide range of
missions and powers bestowed upon them by God.
No matter what purpose they have, their presence
in our lives is still a blessing from God."*
— Sharon R. Wells

Sexual abuse is an ongoing epidemic that destroys lives while leaving a residue of unrelenting hopelessness along the way. The physical act of abuse is agonizing for the victim, but the depth of emotional scarring caused by the infliction of pain can be felt long after the incident occurs or after the physical scars have healed. Victims often emotionally and mentally relive the abuse which causes a trickling down effect in other areas of their lives; this makes the victim feel helpless to combat the resurfacing pain. One way to fight this growing problem among victims of abuse is by speaking up and out, using our voice as a weapon of defense against our attackers. We need to bring sexual abuse out of the dark and into the light in order to break the vicious cycle of abuse.

Unfortunately, it's not always easy to have the courage to step up and point fingers at those who have abused us. The reality is that sexual abusers, more often than not, prey in their comfort zone; coveting that which is convenient and familiar. In many cases, the subjects of desire are people who have let the perpetrator into their life by either blood or by choice. They can be our closest relatives, friends or neighbors, people we know and love.

By the time I reached puberty, I'd been sexually molested three times by three different abusers. I was robbed of the time in life where I should have been enjoying the wonderment and carefree existence of being a

1

child. Instead, I was forced into adult activities and choices. My abusers had not looked beyond their own selfish desires and needs long enough to give thought to the life-long scars they were causing me to physically and mentally endure.

I experienced many years of mental anguish before I could overcome the demons in my head and find inner peace. However, now I can thank God that through intense psychological and spiritual healing therapy, I have been able to finally take control of my life and have begun to heal. My heart can now forgive my abusers. Much more importantly, I have forgiven myself for what I thought I did to cause the abuse to happen in the first place. I am finally at a place where I no longer blame myself for what was done to me. Sadly enough, being victimized by any type of abuse robs the victims of their right to be carefree, healthy and otherwise happy. In many cases, the victim feels guilty, and they suffer in shame. The emotional aftermath and issues that occur can last for the rest of their lives. There is hope, however, if the victim seeks help.

Having been a victim of sexual abuse, I now realize that the abuse robbed me of the healthy, positive self-image that was always my birthright. It also stripped me of my dignity and left me with feelings of guilt and shame. I felt unworthy of being treated like a normal human being. There have been many times when I've wanted to crawl out of my own skin because of the repulsive and degrading feelings I had about myself.

For many years, I used drugs to help me temporarily escape the thoughts and memories that were tormenting me. When the lure of drugs no longer suppressed those embedded wounds, I had no choice but to surrender my life to God. I had to become completely ready to put the drugs and self-destructive behavior I practiced every day behind me.

It was time for me to learn how to love myself.

God is so patient and loving, always willing to give His children the space they need to grow, even when He knows we are unaware of the things we do. He waited for me and kept me safe during my periods of uncertainty. When I was ready to listen, He spoke, giving me all the courage I needed to face my biggest battles and fears. Even more important, He stood in the shadows and loved me until I had the strength and courage to love myself. He proved Himself to be a magnificent and loving God, revealing the fact that if we have trust in Him, He will always guide and protect us.

He mended the broken wings of my shattered soul, molded me into a vessel for His good; a beacon of light showing His wisdom. He is ultimately using me as a tool to share my story for the purpose of giving hope and power to all those who still suffer in silence. I never knew my purpose in life and never understood why I was put here on earth; until the day that God's voice instructed me to minister and be a blessing to others. It was at that time that my life had meaning, my abuse had definition, and my purpose was revealed.

I pray that you will find comfort and courage in the pages herein, and that you will come to know and feel deep within your spirit that God's always loving and never-changing hands are always around and upon you. He will allow your soul to be healed, your mind to be freed and your spirit to soar!

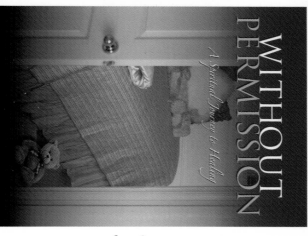

WITHOUT PERMISSION

A Spiritual Journey to Healing

Sharon R. Wells

Angel Wings Publications Announces A New Release!

Without Permission
A Spiritual Journey to Healing
Author, Sharon R. Wells

Without Permission is a gift of hope. It's a source of deliverance for those in need of encouragement that they can move beyond being a victim to becoming victorious.

This journey is a testimony illustrating that tears don't have to last always and strength and healing comes from breaking the silence of abuse. Sharon R. Wells takes the taboo issue of sexual abuse from a position of guilt and shame, transforming it to a position of empowerment stemming from the perception and acknowledgment of self acceptance and community awareness.

Purchase on
Angel Wings Publications website:
www.angelwingspublications.com
(major credit cards accepted)
$15.00 per copy + tax and shipping

Available on Amazon Kindle,
Barnes and Noble Nook &
LuLu.com (e-book)
($9.99 on these websites)

Published by:
Angel Wings Publications, LLC
P.O. Box 96
Vauxhall, NJ 07088
877.713.8298
www.angelwingspublications.com

Angel Wings Publications, LLC

Author, Sharon R. Wells

PART I

SHARON'S STORY

Chapter One

I Surrender

*"Insanity – Doing the same thing over and over
again and expecting different results."* — *Albert Einstein*

A melancholy-filled darkness engulfed the room, suffocating an otherwise normal existence. The sound of my heart pounding to an unrecognizable beat echoed in my ears instead. I curled myself into the instinct-driven, fetal position of comfort, as soon as I got in bed. As much as I hated to admit it, I was too terrified to move.

I pressed my hand against my chest in a vain effort to slow down both my heartbeat and anxiety. *What if I'm having a heart attack?* I thought to myself in what seemed to be a reoccurring rhetorical question. Just like every other night, the thought would not stop bombarding my mood and my mind.

Opening my bedroom window just a crack, I allowed the rainy, windy night air to surround me. The chilly wind outside my window found the force to whip through my room throwing my curtains halfway across my bed. Despite the weather, comforting or destructive, I still seemed to hear voices in the street. I checked the clock again. 3:15 A.M. *What if someone breaks in and kills me?* My pessimistic attitude was in the control seat, leading the way and controlling all of my thoughts.

Far-fetched?—I knew that. I also knew the voices, although audible, might well be products of my imagination…and the fear? I knew where that came from, too. They both were instigators, pushing me to a place I did not want to return to. I exhaled and vowed once more to kick the cocaine habit that was destroying my life. Almost half a gram is how much I snorted each night. A short-lived high followed by a night of hell—the face of insanity! What part of me needed, wanted, pursued this terror, these strange, sick feelings?

I checked the clock again. 4:39 A.M. Time was getting away from me. I had no sense of the hour that had just passed. Nights flew by quickly, as I lay in my bed, lonely and frightened with my heart pounding out of control.

Moments later, the birds began to chirp, and I saw daylight peeking through my blinds. I hated seeing the sun come up because it meant another day at work trying to make it until the end of the day; same routine, different day, nothing special.

I followed a strict rule in my life. I always finished all the cocaine I had each night. I'd vowed never to take it to work. I also refused to leave any in the house. I never, ever, wanted my daughters to find it.

That's why I did whatever was necessary to finish every bit of the coke, no matter how long it took, how late it got, or how intense the high. I generally finished the last of it somewhere between one and two in the morning, which meant another day with no sleep at all. That was my nightly ritual, and I rarely swayed from it. I was all too aware of the paranoid feeling that always accompanied the addiction that was running and destroying my life.

Tomorrow...tomorrow will be the day I stop. Tomorrow I'm really going to do it. Tomorrow I will get this monkey off my back.

I made that vow through all those terrible, paranoid, sleepless filled nights. However, I never followed through. When I finally reached the conclusion that I never would, I changed my routine, adding sleeping pills or alcohol; every downer possible to counteract the cocaine high.

You need to sleep at least for an hour or two so you can function at work. You can't afford to lose your job.

My mind tried to be the voice of reason, but there was no rationalizing with the addict in me.

Despite the fear, despite the paranoia, despite all of my best intentions, the downers didn't work. No matter what drugs I used, I continued to lay awake tossing, turning and praying for just an hour of sleep, most nights.

I dragged myself to the bathroom each morning and did my best to avoid looking in the mirror. I didn't want to see my face because I knew sadness and misery would be staring back at me from their hiding place within my own eyes. I knew the drugs were beginning to take a toll... they had to. That's what drugs do. They kill the user from the inside out; physical deterioration is the first sign. My once smooth complexion was beginning to be scarred with penetrating holes and piercing indentations. That was from the drugs; skin was not created to endure prolonged chemical abuse. Beauty had been one of the things I prided myself on for many years, but with each toxic substance I put in my body, I could see it was just a matter of time before the drugs would steal that away from me too.

Suddenly, my world changed. I got up one morning and knew I couldn't endure another day of hurting myself and living a double life. Trying to appear normal during the day and getting high at night had become much too hard to maintain. Getting my hands on drugs every day was yet another problem. It had never been easy, but it was getting harder every day.

What little faith I had before I started using, the drugs had already taken that from me. Cocaine had been my God—my only God—far longer than I wanted to admit. Like an epiphany of deliverance, the day arrived when I realized I couldn't continue down the road I knew would eventually cost me my life.

Miserable—even desperate as I was, it wasn't easy surrendering my life back to God. I was just so tired of pulling the covers over my head hoping to block everything out. The fact that my sad excuse of existence was normal to me, and that I was comfortable with the way I was living was even more devastating. As if a light bulb went off inside my brain, illuminating the errors of my ways, I realized that as long as I refused to turn my will and my life over to a power greater than me, I was doomed to keep on repeating the same vicious cycle over and over again; a cycle that never failed to send me to the same dark, lonely place of self-hatred and self-destruction. My mind finally accepted the fact that I had to have

9

a strong faith in God in order to allow Him to be the compass that would help me to change direction and get back on the right path.

Although I knew using drugs would also result in financial ruin, unhealthy relationships and depression, I continued with my guilty pleasure over and over again, as a slave to its control. I had already completed a few rehab programs, all voluntarily. After each one, life always seemed a bit brighter as I began to feel optimistic about staying clean. After each attempt at rehabilitation, I would attend Twelve Step meetings daily and swear that because of my determination alone, in time I would succeed. Each time, my attendance at meetings gradually fell off, and before I knew it, I was using again.

However, the day of my epiphany was different. I'd come to the deep and definite realization that determination alone was not enough to keep me clean. God was the only one who could guide me as I journeyed deep inside my heart to find an address the issues that had kept me in pain and threatened to take everything; my children, my job and my life itself.

I knew learning how to love myself would be the toughest battle of my life, but with God in my heart, always with me, I felt ready to try.

That night, I got on my knees and lifted my hands to the heavens. I prayed to God to remove my drug obsession and end my sick, desperate need to get high. I held my hands high as a sign of humble surrender to show God how serious I was as I let the tears stream down my face uncontrollably.

An undeniable sense of peace and calm quickly came over me. I took that as a sign of God's confirmation that He'd heard me. My tears turned into sobs even as I praised God; suddenly, I knew I was going to be okay.

Chapter Two

The Journey Back

"Sometimes we must journey back to our past in order to step in to our future." — Sharon R. Wells

I settled back in my chair and let out a sigh of pure contentment. Sitting on the porch of the house that I had just rented, which was right across the street from the house where I had grown up in, filled me with both pleasure and pain. I took a deep drag off my cigarette and smiled as the vapors filled my lungs, instantly calming my nerves. Thirty-three years had passed and yet, here I was, back on Hunt Avenue again. It was a bittersweet moment. A lot of good memories lived in this small New Jersey town; side by side with some very painful ones as well.

The neighborhood looked pretty much the same as I remembered, except for the addition of a few new houses. The field behind my old childhood home had changed drastically into a very busy Route 78 Highway. Cement roadways covered the grassy fields where I used to play. A sign that time had significantly changed.

It was nice to see that a few of the families that I remembered from my childhood still lived on the block. Mr. Bishop and his family were one of the first families to move to Hunt Avenue. He still lived in the same house, but was now alone because his wife had passed on. A fat cigar hung from his lips, clenched between his teeth, and he had the same jolly personality that I had always remembered. I smiled as I thought, *some things never change!* Even the Mitchells still lived down the block. I enjoyed so many sleepovers with Dawn, Nikki and Keely. They were a family that welcomed me into their home and treated me just like I was a part of their family.

I leaned back, closed my eyes and took a journey down memory lane to the good old days. I remembered how every night right before bedtime. I'd prop myself up on my bedroom windowsill, so I could gaze up at the stars as they sparkled brilliantly against the night sky. Night time was always a time of peace and pleasure as I leaned out of the window and did my best to spot the *Big Dipper*. Life was pure and innocent then. The world was my playground, and I was its child. I could do anything I wanted to do and be whoever I wanted to be.

Remembering those lovely nights, I smiled, realizing what a blessing it was that I had signed the rental lease that day. I had phoned the owner the minute I had seen the "For Rent" sign and realized I could afford it.

However, I also remembered how my heart dropped when the owner said she was in the process of leasing it to someone else. All I could do was talk to God—and I did. I prayed as hard as I could that somehow He would bless me with the house anyway.

The owner called me two weeks later to see if I was still interested in leasing her place. The deal that she was working on had fallen through, so the place was mine if I wanted it.

I smiled to myself knowing that God answers prayers.

I quickly set up a time to meet her to inspect the property. To my surprise, one of my childhood playmates answered the door. I was thrilled when I found out Monica was the owner's daughter. Even though Monica and I hadn't seen each other in over thirty years, it felt almost as if we had never been apart as we began to reminisce. She told me how she had moved to Georgia but continued to come up to the old neighborhood periodically to visit her grandmother before she died. I had fond memories of her grandmother and was sorry to hear that she had passed on.

My friendship with Monica had always been special. She was the first friend whose features and complexion resembled my own—so much so, that sometimes, I thought we could pass for sisters. I was constantly being teased by kids that told me I looked half white and Monica's coloring was similar to my own. We shared features that would make someone take a second look at us and question our ethnicity. That was a common thread that definitely helped to create a strong bond between us.

WITHOUT PERMISSION

Whenever I knew Monica was in town, I would race to her grandmother's house as fast as I could. Then arm in arm, we would rush over to the empty field where we would swing each other around in circles until we got dizzy. That's how happy we were to see each other. Then we would usually spend the rest of our time together jumping rope and playing with dolls.

Other times, we just sat side by side listening to the soothing sounds of the world around us, enjoying each other's company without saying a word. That's the sign of a true friendship; when you can sit in silence with a friend without feeling awkward.

I never asked Monica if people teased her about being light-skinned. I just assumed we shared the same treatment and that experience of ridicule is why we understood each other so well. I was always sad when she had to go home; it was as if a part of me left with her each time she had to leave. Knowing that I would see her on her next visit gave me something special to look forward to.

After viewing the house, Monica and I enjoyed the rest of the afternoon reminiscing about the old days. Within a few short hours, we caught up on everything we had done since the last time we were together. When I signed the lease that day, I had no doubt that God had answered my prayers. I still believe the most important reason for that feeling was the fact that I never told Monica how much our friendship had meant to me.

Looking back, I had come to believe that God sent Monica to me, when I was a child, to reassure me that I wasn't alone in this world. There were others that felt what I felt and experienced what I experienced. It was that same loving hand of God that had put Monica back in my life. He constantly gives us what we need, even if we don't know we need it.

As I sat in my new rental, I realized God had placed me in that house in order for me to take a long look at my childhood; something I knew I needed to do in order to start my healing journey. My childhood, after all, was the time when the seeds of my wounds had first been planted.

I had put off looking at that time in my life because it was just too painful for me to go through mentally. I had avoided it like the plague.

However, finally daring to look back, even just a little, I began to realize that as a child, I was so unsure of who I was and where I belonged. The only self-image I could develop was a negative one; unfortunately, that was the one I had carried into adulthood.

As an adult, self-destructive habits soon became comfortable for me because in the deepest place of my heart, I didn't feel worthy of my existence. That's why I struggled through life, allowing my circumstances to have their way with me, dictating my every thought, every feeling, every move and every decision.

It wasn't until I turned forty that I finally got the courage to take a long look at what was destroying me and categorize how I had gotten to that point. I had made several attempts to clean myself up, but at that point, I knew I had no choice—nothing was going to get better until I faced my past. I had to take a long look at everything that had hurt me and then address those hurts, one by one.

I thought of the saying: *If nothing changes, nothing changes.* Everything stays the same unless we do something to change it. God had positioned me exactly where He wanted me to be in order for me to do the deep-cleansing, gut-wrenching, soul searching I needed to do.

My new home was so close to old memories, which made me think of when my parents and I first arrived in Vauxhall, New Jersey in August, 1968. At the time, I thought it resembled one of the little towns down south where my grandparents had been raised. There were virtually no sidewalks in Vauxhall, for one thing, and many houses were surrounded by thick woods just like the ones down south. That's why I was not surprised when I found out that most of the families who lived here had indeed come from the south.

Vauxhall was peaceful too, much more than Philadelphia where we lived before moving. Birdsongs, the locusts' buzz and the low hum of airplanes in the distance; all those sounds soothed me that first summer. I loved the sweet scent of the wildflowers that grew all around my house. Farmhouses, barns and fields were an important part of the landscape here, too, since Vauxhall was still home to many farms. I knew right away

14

that adjusting to living there would pose a challenge since it was very different from the life I led in Philadelphia.

When I lived in Philadelphia, I would close my eyes when I heard the blaring sirens that never failed to terrify me; the sounds of police cars, ambulances and fire trucks that were always zooming back and forth down the block.

If I was out on the street when the sirens blared, I'd run and hide near the first house I came to, wrapping my arms around myself as tight as I possibly could. Then I would close my eyes and hope the piercing sounds would stop quickly, even though I would continue to shiver in fear, and my ears would ring long after the hated blaring had stopped. I didn't know then, that the terror of the sirens echoing in my ears would turn out to be minor compared to the other terrors I was soon to experience. The noises of city life in Philadelphia, while loud and anxiety filled; were less traumatizing than the groping hands and lustful actions of those residing in Vauxhall.

Chapter Three

My Guardian Angel

*"Angel of God, my guardian dear, to whom His love entrusts
me here, ever this day be at my side to light and
guard, to rule and guide. Amen."*
— *Guardian Angel Prayer*

Idella Woods was the first person to give me and my family a warm welcome in New Jersey. I loved the fact that our house was nestled against the woods, almost as if hidden on Hunt Avenue. The succulent grapes from the grapevine in the backyard were so juicy, you could eat them right off the vine, which we often did. Our house was a cozy dwelling which was the home for Ms. Woods and her two sisters who lived on the first floor. My parents and I lived upstairs on the second floor.

Ms. Woods was a light-skinned older woman with a soft voice, freckles and a warm and friendly personality. She had a welcoming smile and a way of making everyone feel comfortable, like they were family, even if they were strangers to her. She was also the primary care giver for her two sisters, both of whom were very sickly. Ms. Wright, the middle sister, spent most of her time in bed because she had trouble walking. In the evenings, I would sneak ever so quietly from our house down the back stairwell that led to their apartment just so I could visit with Ms. Wright.

Most of the time, I'd sit on her bed and we would talk for hours. She seemed to enjoy the company and so did I. Her good humor and quick wit always kept me laughing, and sometimes she'd even sneak and give me a swig of her *Vicks Formula 44* cough syrup. She never seemed to have a cold, but she drank from that bottle all the same, cold symptoms or not.

After the first swig of the syrup, I knew why. It was heavenly. I liked the way the syrup tasted and the woozy feeling it gave me. I knew then that prevention of colds was not the reason Ms. Wright took more than one capful at a time.

She had Arthritis, and whenever she needed to stretch her legs because the pain became more than she could bear, she'd get out of bed and walk, with the aid of a walker. Ms. Wright's slippers made a rhythmic swishing sound as she moved across the room, one slow and careful step at a time. The squinting of her eyes as she walked made it obvious that mere baby steps caused her a significant amount of pain. I couldn't help but admire her strength in trying to keep mobile in spite of her agony.

The last sister was Ms. Minerva, and she was the eldest of the three. I always thought she resembled an Indian due to her long black braids, which were parted down the middle and twisted with love. She had a natural beauty that seemed as if Mother Nature had kissed her when she was born. She positioned her wheelchair so that it faced her bedroom window, allowing her to look out on to the street and watch the neighborhood. She never said much, she kept to herself and just stared. That was the reason I always wondered what she was thinking as she looked out the window. One day I pulled up a chair next to her hoping to strike up a conversation. I sat there patiently, eagerly hoping and waiting for her to acknowledge me and open up to me about her life or just anything in general; but she still didn't say too much, she barely spoke. I repeated my action of sitting around, waiting for her to talk a few more times and strived for the patience necessary, as I waited for the day she would finally have something to say to me. Eventually, after not getting much attention from her, I just gave up and stopped trying.

It slowly dawned on me that I shouldn't take Ms. Minerva's actions personally; they had nothing to do with me. It was just her way. She treated everyone the same. I noticed that when her grandchildren came to visit, every few weeks or so, she never said much to them either. I think the stroke she had robbed some of the life out of her. She seemed to have lost the will, ability or desire to connect with people. It was nothing personal it was just the way she was. Even with her being the person she was, the cold outer shell of a human being, I still enjoyed when her grandchildren were visiting her. It was always nice to have other kids around to play with.

Some evenings when I made my way down the back stairwell to the apartment, Ms. Woods and I would snuggle up on her couch. I would wrap myself in a blanket as we watched the news together. We would have a special treat of whatever cake or pie she baked earlier that day. Ms. Woods was a good cook, which was one of the reasons I visited her daily. She had a way of "putting her foot" in everything she cooked. My favorite was her sweet potato pie; every bite just seemed to melt in my mouth. I could always tell that she was baking from the wonderful aromas that rose from the first floor, up through the walls, to our house. Ms. Wood's three-tier coconut cake was another one of my favorites. The vanilla ice cream she served on top of her cakes and pies, made them even better; another reason I looked forward to spending time with her and her sisters. Those three women, in one way or another, made our house a home.

Soon after we moved into our new home, my dad introduced me to two cousins whom I had never met before. The field between our houses was the quickest way for me to see them, whenever I felt the need to. Tammy and Junior were just a year and a half apart in age. Their father, Uncle Jasper, was my dad's uncle. His stern demeanor put me off right away, but Aunt Marcia, their mother, was one of the sweetest ladies I had ever met. I thought the glasses she wore made her look like a school teacher, and somehow that soothed me. Since Tammy, Junior, and I was all too young to start school; their grandmother watched all three of us every day.

My mother would drop me off there in the mornings on her way to work, and I would spend the day with my cousins and their grandmother. Being an only child, in the beginning, I loved the chance to be around other kids and the fact that they were family, made it even better. However, my cousins seemed to love doing mischievous things like letting the bathroom sink overflow or putting scotch tape on my neck, then quickly ripping it off as the hair on my neck stuck to the tape, and I screamed in agony. They were treacherous in that regard. They also thought it was funny to blame me for their own naughty deeds. They giggled with pleasure as they watched their grandmother scold me for things she thought I did, but which they had really done. That seemed to fill them with delight, and I grew tired of the guilt by association treatment.

I soon reached the point where I didn't want to face another day of dealing with their tortuous ways. Getting me to cooperate every morning to go to their house became increasingly hard for my mother. I would scream to the top of my lungs each morning while holding the hand rail as tightly as I could for leverage. I tried my best to halt any attempts of going inside my cousins' house. My mother had to peel my hands off of the hand rails and plead with me to go inside where I would have to stay for the day. Having to adjust to that situation was not easy for me, but I had no choice—there was no one else who could watch me. Each morning, I missed my family back in Philly terribly and wished I could go back there.

I was so miserable during the day with my cousins, so I began to spend more time with Ms. Woods at night just for comfort and a feeling of normalcy. One day, I came up with a great idea and quickly asked her if she could watch me during the day. I pushed the idea to the point of begging, a bit, until she finally gave in and agreed to do it. I was ecstatic about my new arrangement and thrilled that I didn't have to spend another day at my cousins' house.

Ms. Woods' house became my safe haven. The fact that she listened to me, along with being a wonderful cook and baker, made it all the better to be with her all day. She would sit me on top of her kitchen counter and let me taste all the delicious foods that she had made. Looking back, I believe it made her as happy to see me enjoying her cooking, as it made me to eat those wonderful dishes. She had no children of her own, that coupled with her age was the reason she felt like a grandmother to me. One day, I asked permission to call her, *Grandma*. I was glad when she agreed, creating a special and strong bond between us.

When I misbehaved, she would tell me that she was going outside to get a switch to beat my *hind* parts. She threatened me for years about getting a switch out of the yard to show me who was actually the boss, but she never had the heart to do it. Grandma was the most gentle, kindhearted, loving person whom I had ever met. She wasn't part of my family by blood, but she was family, to me, by choice.

Every Sunday morning we went to Zion Hill Baptist church in Newark, New Jersey, where she was a member. Zion Hill was where I started learning more about God. My mother had instilled in me a routine of saying my prayers at bedtime. Unfortunately, I was too young to understand what that routine meant or who I was really praying to. I did as I was taught, but I did not have a real connection with God until grandma took me to Zion Hill. Once she got me through the doors, she made it her mission to get me involved in as many activities as possible. I sang in the church choir, and went on several trips with the church; I enjoyed every minute and was amazed at how good being in church felt to me. I finally felt as if I belonged somewhere. It's funny how you don't know that you are missing out on a vital part of life, until you are exposed to a different way of living it.

One of my trips with the church was when we went to a Christmas Show at Radio City Music Hall in New York City. I had never been to New York before, and I was mesmerized by the bright lights that twinkled all over the city making the holiday season feel even more special than imaginably possible. It was a child's paradise, and I couldn't help but savor every minute of it. The aroma of roasted chestnuts from the street corner vendors filled our nostrils, and Grandma always bought us a bag to eat on the bus ride home. Whenever I smell roasted chestnuts to this day, I still remember those special times we shared when I was but a child. Almost every good memory from Vauxhall had her in it, in some form or another.

Grandma Woods helped raise two generations of our family, my sister, Rhonda and me. Not to mention, her family members and neighborhood kids that she cared for along the way. She also taught me some important values that I still continue to live by today. Being kind-hearted and compassionate towards others was one of the greatest examples that Grandma Woods lived by.

People are placed in our life for a reason, a season, or a lifetime, or at least that is how the saying goes. For me, Grandma Woods was placed in my life for all three. Sadly, our "season" ended and became evidence of a short "lifetime," when she passed away suddenly, in November, 1990, after a courageous battle with cancer. A woman, who gave her life over to others for as long as I could remember, finally was taken home to be with our Father. I am sure as she crossed over, God said to her, "Well done my good and faithful servant." At the time of her death, I lived in California, so I never had the chance to say an official goodbye to her. I miss her and wish that I had the chance to thank her for being such an important part of my life. I am more grateful then I can ever say for all the things she taught me. She was an angel who took me under her wing and truly made me feel that I lived in a *Home Sweet Home.* I keep fond memories of my precious grandma close to my heart. She was my guardian angel sent from God.

Chapter Four

Harsh Realities

*"The hardest battle you're ever going to fight is
the battle to be just you."* — *Leo F. Buscaglia*

I was six years old when I started Hamilton Elementary School. Hamilton was close enough for me to walk to, but my mother walked me to school, and my father picked me up in the taxi he drove part-time, those first two years. It wasn't until second grade that my parents decided I was old enough to walk to Hamilton by myself. Parents can be over cautious, but in hindsight, their caution was probably necessary.

I had felt safe when my parents walked me to and from school. There is a certain comfort that a child does not realize until later in life, at having your parents hover over you in protective mode.

When it first came time for me to walk to school and home on my own, Larry and Jeffrey, two brothers from my neighborhood, were my escorts. It was nice walking with them; sometimes, their parents gave us a ride. Whether we walked or rode, I always felt safe with them.

Larry and Jeffrey were my first social connections at school, but Jacqueline was my first female friend. We both carried *Julia* lunch boxes. *Julia* was a popular new TV show, at the time, about a nurse played by *Diahann Carroll*. She was the epitome of a black female and the type of woman I wanted to be when I grew up. I lived vicariously through each episode. It was my favorite show. I was glad to find out it was Jacqueline's too.

Our friendship progressed quickly. We spent lots of time together and then one day Jacqueline told me I was the best friend that she ever had and gave me her beautiful silver and turquoise ring to prove it. Small things mean a lot to a child. I wore the ring home that day and proudly showed it to my mother. My mother was not as happy about the gift as I had hoped she would be. "Did Jacqueline have permission to give you that ring?" she demanded to know. Permission—that was something I had never considered. One thing was certain, if Jacqueline didn't have permission to give me the ring, I would have to give it back to her. Why did adults make acceptance so hard? I never understood that.

"I don't know," I admitted to my mother; with that statement, I knew the inevitable was at hand, I gave the ring back the next day. It didn't really bother me, not as long as Jacqueline, and I was still best friends. We continued to play together after school and later that year, we both joined the same Brownies troop.

The Brownies taught us about leadership, connecting with others and helping to make the world a better place. I was proud to wear my brownie uniform, beanie and sash every Tuesday. My sash displayed all the patches I'd earned. Every time I earned a new patch, my mother and I would sew it on together. Being a Brownie was fun, and it helped me to make more friends.

It was during that time as a Brownie, when I first realized how beautiful, even glamorous, my mother was. More than that, she was kindhearted, too, the perfect combination of inner and outer beauty.

Even though my mother worked only part-time at one of the local stores that didn't pay much, she always found a way to give charitable contributions. She always helped people who needed it most. I loved that most of all about her. Her generosity extended to all that came into contact with her, friend or foe. Whenever someone needed help in our family, she was always there to help out and do as much as she could.

Then there were the cupcakes. I loved baking cupcakes with her. My mother had a special way of creating bright-colored icings that made them look very pretty and delicious. I felt so lucky to have her as my mom.

I also began to notice that lots of other women were jealous of my mother. I was proud to see that she never took it personally or allowed *their* insecurities to make *her* bitter, another quality that made her so special to me. She always made an extra effort to make our holidays special, too. Every Easter, she spent hours curling my hair and making sure my Easter dress looked perfect. The fact that I could see how much she enjoyed every minute of the time she spent fussing over me made it a very special time for me too.

The way I looked, not only on Easter but every other day of the year as well, going to school and even out to play, was very important to her. She took great pride in making sure that I was dressed neatly and beautifully for every occasion, even school.

As much as I loved the attention she gave me, I equally dreaded when she fussed with my hair, combing it into two perfect ponytails each day, then saturating them with water and *Bergamot* hair grease, so that they would stay perfectly in place.

"If I don't put enough grease on your ponytails, they'll dry right up and turn into two little puffs," she always said.

What my mother didn't know was I was the only one in school that was so flawlessly dressed, a fact which made me feel like an outcast most of the time. My light skin tone and interracial features made it even worse. Her insistence on the best concerning how I looked was another source of ridicule for cruel and relentless kids, no matter what her good intentions were. It was no wonder, then, that one day, I concluded that many of the kids at school hated me enough to harm me. I worried about that possibility, endlessly, day after day.

Unfortunately, my worst fears were confirmed as the other kids began to tease me, calling me Half-breed, Butter, Casper, Light Bright or any other name they could think of that would make me feel bad about myself. Hamilton School is where I learned my first lessons on how hurtful and cruel children can be as the taunting and teasing went from bad to worse.

I'd always felt alone in school, since I had no siblings or other close family members there. At some point, other girls began to challenge me, daring me to fight them. I did my best to defuse all those dares and challenges as best as I could.

When that didn't work, I tried talking my way out, making sure they knew I didn't want to fight. When I realized they still wanted to kick my butt, I did what any smart girl would do; I hauled off, running as fast as I could each and every day after school, until I got home safely.

Perhaps because I could see the way the other women's jealousy affected my mother, I suspected the girls might be jealous of me in the same manner—that was why they hated me so much! I also realized how much my mother's insistence that I always look my best for school had backfired. My light skin tones and interracial features may have been at the root of my problems, but my extra-special wardrobe and perfect grooming always made it worse. I didn't belong, I concluded. My mother's efforts to ensure that I was flawless caused others to hate me. I felt like an outcast in every sense of that word.

I kept my eye on the big wall clock when I was in my classes too. I couldn't help but focus and listen as each minute softly clicked by. Every day felt like an eternity. I could barely focus on my studies or the class work of the day. I was too busy worrying about what would happen when I walked home alone, with no one to protect me. I would jump up out of my seat the moment the dismissal bell rang. I was always the first one out of the door, bobbing and weaving my way through the hallway. My heart raced as I looked for the nearest exit, my best shot at avoiding the kids who were always lying in wait, threatening to tear me apart.

I had my first bad day early in the school year. School had just let out, and I was walking home as fast as I could, when a group of boys approached me. One of them hit me in the arm with a crabapple that was as hard as a rock. I watched in horror as my arm swelled up and turned an angry, painful shade of red. The crabapple incident soon turned out to be minor, compared to the day when Boobie Johnson. The biggest and baddest boy in school attacked me. That was the worst day of my life up until that point.

It was a winter day cold enough to send chills down my spine as I walked to school that morning. I was having lunch in the cafeteria when Boobie, a fifth-grader with a serious bad-boy reputation, called me *white girl* and pulled my hair. Boobie's real name was Mark, but nobody called him that, probably because they were too afraid to. Boobie, who was best-known for making trouble, had teased me about my light skin all year even as he threatened to rip me apart. As much as I hated him and his threats, I never thought he meant it, not until that horrible day.

I was terrified as I kept looking up at the big wall clock in the classroom; I always dreaded walking home alone. The minute the dismissal bell rang; I jumped up out of my seat and bolted for the door. I bobbed and weaved my way through the hallway as I taught myself to do, then my heart raced, as I set my eyes on the nearest exit. My heart raced faster the moment I ran out and saw all the kids that had already gathered outside waiting for my arrival; the crowd got bigger by the minute. Bad news traveled fast, apparently.

I began to run as fast as I could, careful not to slip on the ice patches on the sidewalk. My red scarf blew in the wind, slapping me across the face with the bitterness of the climate outside and with the possibilities that lay ahead. I hadn't gotten far when I realized my cheeks were ice cold, and I was running out of steam. I couldn't catch my breath either. Suddenly, I felt a stabbing pain in my side, and I knew I had no choice but to slow down.

I couldn't stop the panic I felt when I turned and saw that group of kids—a parade of kids, gaining on me! Boobie led the way. They moved closer and closer as I just stood there, short of breath and frozen with fear.

Then it happened—Boobie caught me! He came right up to me and shoved me as hard as he could as the other kids cheered him on. I was trapped and defeated, too small to fight him back and too terrified to move from the position I held. He pushed me again, forcing me down onto the ice where I slipped and fell, hitting my face so hard it brought tears to my eyes.

I noticed the rip in my tights and the bloody scrape on my knee, as I struggled to get up. The kids were still circled around me, laughing, screaming and pointing at me like I was some kind of freak of nature.

I was almost upright when Boobie grabbed my legs and forced me down again, then he pulled down my tights in front of everyone, exposing my panties for all to see. I got up and pulled my tights up as fast as I could, then I began to cry and run, looking for a red hand house; a house with a picture of a red hand in the front window. The red hand signified which houses were safe if a child was in trouble. As soon as I'd started having problems at school, I had located all the red hand houses in the neighborhood and memorized where they were. That day, I knew I was only six houses away from the closest one.

I was gasping for breath, by the time I reached it. My heart felt like it was pounding out of my chest as I frantically began to ring the bell. It felt like a long time before an older woman opened the door and gestured me inside, but the reality dictated that it was less than a minute. She looked at me warmly; I could tell she cared about what was happening to me. I could see it in her eyes. True care for another cannot be hidden when one looks into the eyes of the soul.

"What happened to you, dear?" she asked her voice soft and gentle.

When I told her of the mob that was after me, she offered to call my mother at work to be the Calvary for me. I began to calm down as soon as I heard my mother's voice. She was leaving work, so she could come pick me up at Miss Violet's house.

I realized then that the woman at the door was named Violet, a perfect name, for the sweet and lovely disposition that she had. Miss Violet had helped me and the worst was over. My mother picked me up a short time later. The next day, she and my father went to the school to tell the principal what Boobie had done. The school contacted Boobie's parents, and he was reprimanded for it. I was so glad when Boobie stayed far away from me after that. Suddenly, I felt safe. The red hand home had worked for me.

However, the attack was still traumatic. It was the beginning of the downward spiral of my self-esteem. If I had been ashamed of the girl I was before Boobie pulled my tights down; that same shame increased a hundredfold after that moment, as I realized all the taunting and the teasing confirmed the fact that I was more than just different—I was an outcast. When I asked myself how I had earned that title, the answer came quickly; there must be something wrong with me.

I didn't know then that my poor self-image was about to become a self-fulfilling prophecy.

Chapter Five

Secrets of Summer

"Trust is like a mirror, once it has been broken you will never see it the same way again." — Sharon R. Wells

L ife didn't get any easier for me at home or in school the following year. In retrospect, I realize that our childhood years are the most impressionable and critical years in anyone's life. With every experience we have, it has a way of molding us into the person we become later in life. Whether it's good or bad, healthy or dysfunctional; those experiences become the potter, and we are merely the clay.

The biggest challenge I faced at home was from the other kids that mercilessly taunted me about my skin color while insisting that my stepfather couldn't be my real father because my biological father absolutely HAD to be white. My mixed looks became the basis for daily abuse and ridicule. Children can be cruel to one another. That's a fact of life, and I was bullied and abused by other kids from sun up to sun down.

Luckily, for me, there were four kids that lived next door to me; three girls and a boy. The two older sisters took me under their wings, as if I were part of their family. They taught me how to stand up for myself and fight back when I had to. I eagerly watched like a boxing intern, while they showed me how to hold my two fists up in front of me in protection mode. Then, as if they were heavy-weight trainers, they moved on to stage two and taught me several punching and jabbing moves and techniques. They explained the rules of survival stating that if I learned how to fight, I would be able to defend myself if the need arose. That acquired knowledge and skill would help keep me safe. They preached it daily and I inhaled every word.

In fact, I tried as hard as I could to do my best, whenever I practiced the defensive moves they taught me. Reality dictated that I really wasn't a fighter in any sense of the word. So, no matter how good I was in practice, when someone challenged me, face to face, in school or on the street, nine times out of ten, I just froze. All my training went out the window when the rubber met the road.

It was always a bad situation with kids challenging me all the time, threatening to whip my butt if I didn't fight back. With no choice but to accept the challenge, I always gave the physical battles my best shot. One by one, in one way or another, I failed to win.

The racial tension, floating in the air at the time, made the fact of me having light skin an even worse scarlet letter to all whom looked at me. The Newark, New Jersey riots occurred just a few years earlier, and were recent enough that the memories of that terrible time were all too clear and fresh in my mind. Fear engulfed me.

To this day, I can still remember how it felt when my cousins and I had to hide on the floor of my Aunt Marcia's car when she drove through Newark. The pungent odor of gunpowder around us is another memory that will stick in my mind until the day I die.

I still can visualize the burnt-out shells of buildings on Springfield Avenue in the heart of the city. Even though a few years had passed since the riots, the anger born of racism still ran high—which made it a particularly difficult time for a light-skinned girl like me with Caucasian features.

It took me a while to build up my courage, but I finally asked my mother if my real father had, indeed, been white. Since my stepfather was the only father I had ever known, it hadn't occurred to me to ask her that question before. My uncontrollable need to know got the best of me, and I couldn't fight it any longer. The fact that I knew my step father had legally adopted me, closed the deal in my mind. As far as I was concerned, my stepfather was my real father, my only father, in every sense of the word. He was the only man I could call, 'dad,' but I still had a desire to trace my genes back to the point of my conception.

"Your biological father, I won't call him your 'real' father because he was never that; but 'yes' he was a black man. He left me when I got pregnant, and never looked back." My mother replied as if uttering the words out loud pained her. I remember nodding and saying something appropriate, then going to my room to feel the feelings—a wide range of them, all uncomfortable. First, her answer disappointed me. Hearing her say my natural father was white would have made more sense to me. Her stating he was black just added confusion and frustration for me. I was confused because, if my father really was a black man, why did I look so white? That question took control of my mind and held it hostage.

I also wanted to know why the man who fathered me had found it so easy to walk out on us. Was my mother unlovable? Was I? Was that why all the other kids insulted me, threatened me, and challenged me to fight them? Did they sense my unlovable factor and use it to their benefit? Would any of it ever change? Would anyone ever accept me? Would anyone ever love me?

The questions came fast and furious. However, I did not have the answer to any of them.

As grateful as I was for my relationship with my stepfather, I still couldn't stop asking myself the hard-hitting questions I yearned to have answered. I couldn't help but wonder about the man responsible for giving me life. I tried hard to make the distinction in my head between the sperm donor and the man who raised me. My stepfather was a hard-working man with a big, sometimes intimidating, presence. It took a while for me to warm up to him when he first came into my life, but we became quite close after that.

I loved the feeling of being his little girl, a feeling that was especially important in light of the way the other kids treated me. I needed the security of having that safe spot in my heart. My stepfather and I enjoyed going places together on the weekends. When the weather was nice, we loved to go to Weequahic Park in Newark to watch the baseball games. I wasn't the son whom I think all fathers wish for, but we were inseparable even when it came to sports. The Raiders, a team made up of my father's co-workers, played baseball at Weequahic Park every weekend, and he loved to bring me there to help him cheer them on.

He and I also enjoyed fishing. I didn't catch many fish, whenever we went, but that didn't bother me or him. We would spend the whole day together and that is what mattered. We were alike in a lot of ways, and our only differences seemed to stem from his views on disciplining me when I had done something wrong. My mother's spankings didn't scare me at all. They didn't hurt for one thing. I also felt fairly sure that they hurt her more than they hurt me.

My stepfather took a different approach when it came to disciplining. When he caught me misbehaving, he sent me to get his dark brown belt. The one made of thick leather, which never failed to instill fear in my heart just by looking at it. My hands shook when I gave the belt to him and with good reason. I knew its possibilities, and he tore my butt up with that belt, beating me hard until I thought for sure it would never end.

As any child would, I hated his discipline. It was always over the top and unwarranted from my point of view at the time; but that was my thinking from a child not wanting to pay the piper for my bad behavior. Nor did I think it was the right way to discipline a child. Looking back, I realize his beatings established a balance between love and discipline, teaching me never to take anything in life for granted and impressing on me the need to take responsibility for my actions. His discipline also taught me I had to work hard for what I wanted.

That year, with things so difficult at school, the beatings just made everything even worse. The teasing and taunting were the worst they had ever been. Looking back, I know now that every threat, every insult, every mean word and every stroke of my father's belt, added that much more momentum to the downward spiral of my self-esteem.

At some point, I began to try to boost my self-esteem and the acceptance of others by trying to buy friends by giving them candy. *Squirrel Nuts, Penny Candies, Pixie Sticks* and *Bazooka* bubble gum were among the most popular candies that year. Many kids couldn't buy those candies at all, since they didn't have an allowance for things like that. I felt lucky that I got enough allowance to buy them candy. I wasn't too surprised when I learned later that all those candy-induced friendships lasted only as long as the candy did.

I was proud of the fact that despite all the problems and the alienation from kids in general, I still made good grades and succeeded in making a few real friends. Working hard to build my confidence, I decided to try playing a musical instrument. I chose the cello, which looked like a giant violin that stood taller than I did. I loved the sound it made, which was the reason why I was so excited to haul it home from school. I showed my parents and all they could see was the size of the cello. They quickly suggested a smaller instrument might be a better choice.

I was disappointed but not disheartened; I dragged the heavy cello back to school the next day and exchanged it for a violin. I was very enthusiastic about learning to play the violin and brought it home every weekend to practice. I loved the way it sounded as I ran the bow across the strings. Even better, the music made me feel good until one Saturday afternoon when the bridge that holds the strings fell off, and I panicked. Afraid to tell anyone what happened, I glued it back with Elmer's glue then returned it to school, praying the teacher wouldn't notice.

I was shaking in my shoes when the music teacher took the violin out of its case and saw the glue drippings all over the beautiful violin. He was furious and so angry that he told me I could no longer practice music in his class. That was the last time I ever tried to play an instrument. I took his action as yet another form of rejection of who I was. Once again, I wasn't good enough to belong.

At the end of every school year, my parents sent me to my grandparents' house for the summer. It was their way of protecting me from being picked on by the neighborhood kids. Being older and no longer afraid of the sirens of the city, I loved being in Philadelphia and spending time with my extended family. My Aunt Beannie, my mother's youngest sister, felt like the big sister that I never had. Aunt Beannie and I have always had a special bond, not to mention how cool I've always thought she was.

The first thing she'd do when I arrived each year, was grab a comb and start corn-rowing my thick, curly, always-tangled hair. One year, she surprised me by buying me a pair of high top sneakers; her way of keeping me in touch with my African American/Philadelphian roots.

The neighborhood was like one big family even though the kids came from a wide range of different nationalities and cultures. We all played together, going from house to house having fun.

We did some very dangerous things too, like jumping from rooftop to rooftop to prove how tough we were. The girls in the neighborhood also taught me how to jump *Double-Dutch*, which I loved. Nights were reserved for games like *Hide and Seek,* and *Tin Can Annie.*

Some of the best times I had were when someone turned on the fire hydrant, the water plug, as we called it in those days. We'd jump around and splash, like it was our own personal community pool. It was great fun until someone from the fire department came and shut it off.

The Waterloo playground was directly across from my grandparents' house. It was there where they gave out free lunches to the neighborhood kids every summer. We'd all run to the playground trying to get there before the lunches were gone. The lucky kids that got there on time were given a sandwich wrapped in plastic, a pint of milk, a container of juice, and a piece of fruit. Waterloo was also the place where I got my first nicks and scars, something that was bound to happen since I was the only girl in the crowd of male cousins. Many days, I'd run back to grandma's house hurting and bleeding. My Aunt Millie kept the first aid kit handy. She knew that I'd need it. Aunt Millie was always so loving and kind, never failing to nurse and comfort me through every nick and scar. I was grateful that she was there because she made me feel like I was her little girl.

My grandmother was a strict disciplinarian that never hesitated to whip our butts when necessary; but she also showed us a lot of love. I guess that's why everyone gathered at her house, where there were always an abundance of close family ties and food. I loved it when she and I spent our own special time together. She'd take me shopping with her to *Kelly's*

Korner, a local department store down on Front Street. On our way back home, she'd buy me a huge pickle to eat. Spending time with her was one of the things I loved most about my summers in Philly.

My grandmother has always been the center of the family. Unfortunately, I didn't see too much of my grandfather. Granddad worked hard down at the shipyard doing as much as he could to provide for his family. When he did come home, I remember him smiling and smoking one of his beloved pipes or cigars. The smell of both still makes me smile. He was always so glad to see all of his grandchildren, and we'd run and jump right into his arms.

He and my grandmother planned a barbeque outing for us every year. My cousins Tonya, Natalie, Ronnie, Michael, Robert and I loved piling into granddad's station wagon to drive to one beautiful park or another. We didn't care if we were all squished in the back seat; we were just excited about getting to the park. Most of the time, the parks were never too far away from the house. We could always tell when we were getting close by the aroma of fresh cut grass. We would lay out blankets once we got there, and then roll around in the sweet-smelling grass playing games and having fun. I always looked forward to having that carefree and fun filled barbeque day. My Aunt Carol would make sure she brought a bushel of crabs. I loved eating crabs with Aunt Carol. She would sit with us and show us how to eat them. "Make sure you don't eat the dead man fingers' part of the crab," she'd say, showing us where it was. She also wrote the most beautiful poetry that she would recite to the family. Uncle Nate, my mother's only brother, was always our deejay and would play us music on his portable stereo. Aunt Mickey and Aunt Jimmie would show us all the latest dances and moves. Each of my aunts had their own unique quality, which made me admire them so much. There was nothing better, to me, then spending time with my family.

As I grew up, I learned that life has a way of tainting even the most beautiful of memories. Amongst all the love that I received from being around my family, the same family environment opened up a path that eventually led to my abuse. My guard was down to the fact that some abusers wear robes of trust. Abusers also hide behind the mask of family or friends.

It was during two separate summer breaks that I was sexually molested by two different men. I was almost eight the first time it happened and barely aware of my changing body. Apparently, others were noticing changes in my body and taking notes for their own pleasure.

I was alone, that first time, with someone I trusted. I didn't think about it too much when he suggested I go with him into the kitchen. I had no reason to be leery of being alone with him; after all, he was a family friend. Once inside the kitchen, I watched in shock, as he leaned against the refrigerator and greased his genitals with *Royal Crown* petroleum jelly. I knew that men and boys had different genitals than I had, but I had never seen a penis before in my life. *Royal Crown* changed all that for me. As he stroked himself using the refrigerator as leverage to hold his body up, I noticed his penis beginning to grow and all I could do was stare, not knowing what to do. I wasn't sure what was going on as he smiled a wicked grin in my direction continuing his up and down strokes applying the jelly on himself. I looked around the kitchen wondering, what, if anything, his actions had to do with me.

Everything became clearer when he positioned me directly in front of him, pulled my panties down to my ankles and slid himself back and forth between my legs. He made grunting sounds, which got faster and louder, as he continued to slide back and forth. After a few minutes, I felt a sticky substance drip down my legs, and then he withdrew from between my legs. It was over.

He said very little to me as he pulled up his pants and reached into his pants pockets. I remember that he was too tall for me to look him eye-to-eye in the face. I do remember that after he was done and pulled up his pants, he cleaned off the substance from my legs with a kitchen towel, pulled up my panties and gave me some change out of his pocket to go to the candy store. The fact that he never told me not to tell anyone about what happened was a given; the money he gave me was payment for my silence. I accepted it shamefully, sure that I must have done something wrong even if I wasn't sure what it was. I tried to make sense of it all as I ran to the corner store. I allowed the blackmailing treats of my molester to silence me.

I knew that what happened was dirty somehow, but I was too young to understand that I had just been molested. I couldn't make the connection in my head. All I knew was that my otherwise carefree summer had just been compromised along with my innocence. I didn't know exactly what secret I was being paid to keep, but whatever it was, I was sure it was shameful. It felt nasty and it made me feel unclean. That was enough for me to know that what happened was not right.

I didn't know the names for male and female genitals, but I knew they were always referred to as private parts. That meant they were private, not to be shown or touched by anyone. My abuser had shown me his private part before—he had seen or touched mine. My gut told me that his doing so wasn't right, which confused me. I had trusted him. Why had he done this? Was it my fault? Did I somehow make him think it was okay to treat me the way he did?

I went back home to New Jersey at the end of that summer, a changed girl with a different perspective on trust. At the age of eight, my view of the world had been tainted. I never told a soul about what happened that day. I saw my abuser a few times during the year when my parents took me to Philadelphia for family visits, but I always acted as if nothing happened. I never said a word.

Even now, many years later, *Royal Crown* petroleum jelly brings back memories I tried so hard to forget. If I succeeded in denying what happened, by burying it in the back of my mind, the sight or smell of *Royal Crown* is still a little trigger, which is always enough to bring it all flooding back to the forefront of my mind.

I was molested again on another summer break about a year later, when I was almost nine. My second abuser was also someone I knew and trusted. I went to his house to visit his sister, but quickly found out he was the only one home at the time. Trusting him because I had known him and his family for a very long time, when he invited me into his bedroom, I went without apprehension.

WITHOUT PERMISSION

Once in his room, I sat on the bed, and we talked for a little bit about nothing in general other than small talk. I was completely surprised when he laid me back and got on top of me. He transformed from a position of being the brother of my friend to a sexual partner. He rubbed his hands all over my body and kissed me, as if I were a willing partner. Feeling shocked and very, very dirty and ashamed for what he was doing to my body, I quickly managed to free myself and get out of the house. I pushed him off of me and ran until my legs and my lungs could no longer deal with the extra exertion on both. I finally made it to a place where I could sit and gather both my breath and my thoughts.

I never told anyone about what he had done. For many years, I also succeeded in blocking the memory of it out of my mind. I didn't put a label on it when it happened. I was too young to give the experience a definition, but in looking back, I realize now that what he did was molest me that day. Although he didn't penetrate me, he violated me in a way I'll never forget. A way that I didn't consent to and one that changed the way I viewed myself. I'm sure, too, that he knew exactly what he was doing at the time he did it. My feelings meant nothing to him. They rarely do when it comes to predators and prey. He got what he wanted, as he took advantage of me in the worst possible way.

Chapter Six

Birth of a Warrior

*"A warrior is someone who has realized her self worth
and is ready to fight for her life." — Sharon R. Wells*

At the end of the school year, I graduated from Hamilton Elementary School. That summer, I saw a *Barbizon* commercial on television, which promised to make someone, anyone, look and feel like a model. I pleaded with my mother to sign me up because I thought that by taking the training I would be on my way to stardom. I believed deeply in their promises. In an effort to keep me involved in positive activities, since I was now spending summers at home, my mother agreed and signed me up to attend. *Barbizon* taught me how to walk like a runway model and prepare for commercial auditions. I thought that I was on my way to becoming the star whom I had only dreamed about becoming—the person who I had fantasized about from my bedroom window. I looked forward to classes on Saturdays, and I loved getting dressed up for them.

After completing the course, my parents and I were hoping that something promising would come out of my experience at *Barbizon*. However, the valuable lessons that I learned were how to walk on a runway and learning to pose for photographs. The runway walking seemed to be most beneficial as I began to strut with an air of confidence. This was something I had not possessed before. It became a natural part of me and the mask that I wore to hide my shame. On the outside, it appeared that I was confident, but really inside there was a little girl who just wanted to be loved and accepted. I knew how to hide my feelings well and be transparent to all that were looking from the outside in. After summer was over and school was back in session, I attended a new school, Central Six, a school just for sixth graders. Each student had graduated from one of the six elementary schools in Union Township. We were all brought together in one school.

Not much had changed for me in the new school, as I was still challenged to fights by my classmates. However, I gracefully declined by running home every day after school as fast as I could, something that I was already use to doing. I was still too afraid to stand up for myself and sprinting home at lightning speed seemed like a much better idea. The task of mapping out my escape route each day had started wearing me down. It was very disappointing knowing that nothing had changed for me. I could have been a track star for my speed and skill in evading others.

My body had just begun developing as I was going through puberty. My breasts were in a weird stage and had begun protruding, which embarrassed me more than I can ever say. They were so noticeable that the boys began calling me, Torpedo. I started putting band-aids over my nipples in an attempt to avoid the unwanted attention. It was at that time when another man whom I had known and trusted for years began sexually molesting me. It started out by what I thought was an innocent kiss of lips just touching until he tried sliding his tongue into my mouth. After the initial sliding of the tongue, he always seemed to want to give me a kiss, whenever he greeted me. He was someone whom my family and I knew and loved very much. I shunned it off and made myself believe that I was imagining what was happening and that molestation was not the case concerning him and me.

Then one day, while I was alone with him, he kissed me again. At that time, not only did he slide his tongue into my mouth, but he fondled my breast too. As his fingers fumbled with my budding breasts, his actions brought back repulsive feelings of those summers spent in Philadelphia. I did not want to believe that the same thing was happening to me all over again. Somewhere in the back of my mind, I knew that things were just the same, only in a different, more grown-up body. I could not respond to his advances, even though I knew what he was doing was wrong. When he touched my body, I froze in the same fear I had before. I wanted to scream, but no sounds would come out of my mouth. I was traumatized by what he was doing to me. He had severed the bond between us. I couldn't imagine what he could be thinking that would allow him to be so selfish in his actions. I felt ashamed and thought that if I told anyone, they would not believe me, so why take the chance on causing myself more shame. There I was once again, having to bury yet another secret and bear more shame. I continued to blame myself. I felt like I must be doing something, which caused men to act in a manner that everyone, even someone of my age, knew to be wrong.

After graduating Central six, I began my first year in middle school; Burnet Jr. High. Rage had already started building up inside of me for not being accepted by peers and for the shameful secrets that I had to bury in the back of my mind. Both were eating away at my spirit and were causing me extreme mental pain. I didn't know how to find comfort, and I was tired of running home each day. I felt it was time for me to start standing up for myself.

There was a feeling stirring inside of me, as if someone was screaming to get out. That person, who I had not even known existed, showed up one day during my gym class in seventh grade. I had gotten into an altercation with one of my classmates over something minor, and before I knew it, we were scuffling outside on the track field. My rage, which had built up over several years was the product of repressed mental and physical abuse, found a way to unleash itself. The person inside of me who had been locked away found a way to emerge from the depth of her hiding place. I blacked out during the fight and all I could remember afterwards were the two teachers who pulled me off of my classmate. When I saw that she had a bloody nose, I knew that I was in big trouble. At that point, I felt bad about my classmate's nose, but it felt good to finally stand up for myself. The new, unfamiliar person from deep inside me was bold, sassy and courageous, the total opposite of me. I welcomed her emergence, it was liberating. It didn't take long before I allowed her presence to take over and let the timid and fearful person whom I was fade into the background. We were one person, but I allowed her to take the forefront and protect us both.

I vowed to no longer be afraid; my perception about the world was that it was a battlefield. I was on guard and ready to attack anyone who I thought was out to hurt me. In my mind, most people were the enemy, and I was ready for war. I kept a serious look on my face and rarely cracked a smile, which quickly became my defense mechanism. I wanted to numb my pain. I was unhappy, and I just didn't want to feel anything anymore.

During my first year in high school, I started hanging out with two girlfriends whom I knew from childhood. We called ourselves the black version of *Charlie's Angels,* and we quickly became the "in crowd." Drugs at school were easy to find, and it wasn't too long before I began experimenting with smoking weed. Marijuana was my first experimentation with drugs, and I was having a great time using it; I liked the way it made me feel. I was able to temporarily forget about my problems and be whoever I wanted to be. It also boosted my self-confidence. I felt courageous enough to stand up to anyone while under its spell, and it wasn't long before I built a reputation as a veteran fighter. That reputation earned my respect from my peers, and I was proud of the new person who I had become.

It was also around that time that I had met my first love, Wali. We met on a blind date which was set up by a mutual friend of ours. Wali was three years older than me and lived in Newark. Newark was known to be a tough city and anyone who lived there was considered to be tough too. For that reason, I found him very attractive; good girls always like bad boys. Everyone knows opposites attract, and Wali and I were no different.

He was handsome, wore fine clothes and had the coolest walk, which we called, "swag." It took a little while for me to warm up to him. However, after several conversations, we realized that we had so much in common, including being born on the same day.

Wali's birth name was Edwin, but he had given himself an attribute, which was the name he used on the street. Giving yourself an attribute was when someone changed their birth name to an Islamic name. During the late seventies, having an attribute was the *in* thing to do. Although many people changed their name, it did not necessarily mean they were of the Islamic faith. I had also given myself an attribute as well, and my name was Shakirah.

Wali was my first real boyfriend and being with him took my mind off of everything that I tried so hard to forget. I never shared with him about being molested. I was too ashamed and thought that if he knew, he may not have wanted to be with me. I thought if he knew my past, he would think I was dirty and not worth his time. I had such a chip on my shoulder that it caused us to fight all the time. No matter how many fights we had, we were inseparable. I loved spending time with him and enjoyed the wonderful dates that he took me on.

While attending high school, I found myself in the principal's office quite regularly, getting suspended for fighting. Things at school may not have changed, but I certainly did! Shakirah was the person who was in charge, and she didn't back down from anyone. I recall my father once saying that he had always told me to protect myself, but that he thought my fighting had gotten out of control.

I started experimenting with more serious drugs during that year. I attended *get high* parties, and it was there where I found a variety of drugs. Someone from school would have a party at their house while their parents were at work. Some classmates would cut school to go, and hoped that their parents wouldn't come home early. It was at those parties where I was introduced to drugs like THC, Hash, Acid and Cocaine as well as many others. Cocaine always seemed to be my drug of choice.

My parents noticed the change in me and saw that my unpredictable behavior was spiraling out of control. It wasn't long before they grew overly concerned because I was not communicating with them. They became frustrated and made an appointment for me to see a psychiatrist hoping to get some answers regarding my anger. They knew I was acting erratically, but they didn't suspect I was using drugs. They also didn't know that I was angry with them because they had not figured out on their own what was troubling me. I refused to open up to the doctor, which my parents eventually realized was a waste of time in trying to pursue. They were not getting any closer to figuring out my problems, and neither was the doctor. After a few more sessions and still no progress being made, my parents canceled the rest of the appointments, and we never went back again.

The pressure of trying to figure out who I was and what I wanted to do with my life was overwhelming. I based my identity on who everyone else thought I should be. Because of my background at *Barbizon*, I thought modeling was something I wanted to do, so I started doing runway modeling for some amateur fashion shows in local areas. People thought that I had a great shot at being a successful print model and that sounded good to me too. Unfortunately, I was not tall enough to be a professional runway model. So, instead I began building a portfolio hoping to land a huge advertisement deal. Deep down, inside, I thought my beauty was my only asset that I could rely on. I didn't realize it then but the reality was that there was a beautiful person inside me who was looking for love in all the wrong places.

At that time, the only thing that mattered to me was staying numb, in order to keep the secrets that were tormenting me buried as far down inside as possible.

Chapter Seven

The Secret Revealed

"Nothing makes us as lonely as our secrets."
— Sharon R. Wells

My abuser, whom I will call John to protect his identity, continued to molest me whenever the opportunity presented itself. I did my best to avoid him in every way possible. Unfortunately, he was so connected to my family and me that it was impossible for me not to have interaction with him. No one in the family had a clue that John was touching my body in places and ways he had no permission to.

John even went so far as to check my private parts to see if I was still a virgin. It was important in his mind that I was. I tried convincing him that my virginity was in tack, but he made it a point of fondling me to inspect for himself. He wanted to make sure I was still pure. Every time John touched me, I sank further and deeper into a black hole. I could never understand why God was allowing me to be a victim in that way. By the time I turned fourteen, concealing the secret of my continuous molestation was tearing me apart inside.

Most of the time, I felt like I wore an invisible sign on my forehead that said "damaged goods." I was convinced the world could see that I was tainted. There were so many times when I wanted to tell someone what was happening or just scream it out so loud that someone, anyone, would make him stop. However, my hidden shame prevented me from doing that. It kept me in a place where I had no idea how to make him stop or how to free myself from his reign.

WITHOUT PERMISSION

The pain from the abuse and from concealing it was so unbearable that my mind often felt like a pressure cooker ready to explode. I felt alone and abandoned, like there was no one to protect me, least of all myself. I experienced a lot of headaches during that time because the burden of my mental distress was overwhelming.

That year, I became enraged and unwilling to continue protecting the man who apparently felt entitled to violate my body, whenever he wanted. One evening, I started praying. I asked God to give me the courage and strength to tell my mother what was happening to me. I knew I could put my trust in her, and I hoped she would believe me.

A few hours later, my prayers were answered. God gave me the strength I needed to make my decision. He told me everything would be okay. He assured me that it was time to stop hiding the source of my pain. Armed with the comfort from above, nothing and no one could stop me from revealing the secret that was causing me so much shame. That night, I waited until everyone was asleep before I tiptoed into my parents' bedroom. I gently tapped my mother's shoulder to wake her. I told her I needed to talk to her about something really important.

Her eyes piqued with curiosity as she slowly rose from her bed. It wasn't an everyday occurrence for her daughter to say she had something important to talk about, and I could feel her motherly concern. Still groggy from being awakened from her sleep, she followed me downstairs. I made sure that I turned the light to the dim setting to hide my face before sharing the most shameful secret of my life.

We sat a few inches from each other on the couch. She was just about to ask me what was wrong, when the words poured out of my mouth like a streaming faucet. I spoke really fast and couldn't control myself. I just wanted so badly to get it out; to say everything before I changed my mind and lost my courage. I shivered in fear as I continued to spill out the horror that I had kept hiding far too long.

Within minutes, I realized I had blurted out the details of my abuse so quickly that it didn't come out exactly the way that I had rehearsed and planned. I looked up timidly to assess my mother's reaction. Her body was limp; she was staring at the wall. Her eyes were empty as she tried to make sense of what I had just told her. The facts had clearly hit her like a ton of bricks.

I will never forget the painful look of disappointment in her eyes. It was a look that can only be compared to hearing that someone had just died. I guess in a way I had, or at least my innocence had, and that fact filled her with sadness. She wrapped her arms tightly around me, pulling me close to her as she tried to fight back the tears that welled up in her eyes. The sweet fragrance she always wore enveloped and comforted me as I melted in her arms, instantly feeling safe for the first time in a long time. She told me how sorry she was for all I had been through and how brave I was for carrying the burden alone. She continued to hold me and listened closely as I shared with her the horrible details of what had been happening to me. As I relived the abuse, the warmth of her body gave me the relief I had been yearning for. I was finally free from the dark secret that kept me in bondage way too long.

I know that what I was telling her was shocking, and she was equally devastated once I revealed the identity of my abuser. John was a man we loved and respected and someone neither of us would have imagined would betray our trust. I could sense that she felt betrayed by John, and I wondered what thoughts and feelings were running through her mind as I continued giving her details of how frequent it occurred. There was anger in her voice when she asked me why I had waited so long to tell her. For a slight moment, I was afraid, but very relieved when she said that her anger was not directed at me. She made it clear that her anger was fueled by her regret for not having been able to end my pain earlier or to stop it from happening in the first place.

My mother's delicate nature had vanished and was replaced with the aura of a defender. From the look in her eyes, I was sure John would pay for hurting me. The last thing I wanted to see was my mother in pain. In fact, I always wanted to protect her. Perhaps, that need to protect her was the main reason I kept my shameful secret to myself for so long. On some level, I thought it was easier for me to carry the burden for everyone, then to have anyone else in the family share my pain.

WITHOUT PERMISSION

That night, I was relieved to see my mother believed everything I told her. Having read about girls in similar situations and seen them interviewed on TV, I knew there were some parents who accused their children of lying. The parents were not willing to face the emotional pain or take the necessary steps to make the abusers incur consequences for their behavior.

I felt not only relieved, but also very grateful when my mother assured me that what happened to me wasn't my fault at all. She added that we would confront my abuser together, as a family. Suddenly, all my fears about sharing my secret were gone. I felt lighter and the pressure cooker in my mind seemed to turn itself off.

I did, however, convince my mother not to involve the police or anyone else. My family and I, like many other victims, chose to deal with the abuse ourselves and hope the pain would go away in time. Like other victims of abuse, we did not want to face ridicule or have to continue to relive what had happened. We just wanted to make sure it stopped and by making it stop, we hoped the healing would begin.

My mother blamed herself for not protecting me better. I know that even to this day, she still continues to carry that burden. I never told her how I'd already been molested two times before John, by two other men in Philadelphia; the last thing I wanted to do was overwhelm her with my history of abuse and molestation. She already carried guilt on her shoulders concerning John; I couldn't bear making that burden heavier by telling her about the others before him. Mainly, I just tried to reassure her that I was okay. That was my way of trying to ease her pain.

I cried that night as I watched her go through emotional pain and guilt, but I didn't shed any tears around her because I didn't want her to see all the pain in my heart. I had become a master at burying my feelings, and I wanted to be strong for her; although revealing my sexual abuse was a cry out for help.

As much as she assured me that the abuse wasn't my fault, I continued to blame myself. The damage was done and the negative opinions I had internalized were there, deep inside me. I questioned if they would ever go away.

Most girls, my age at the time, were experiencing puberty, learning new dances, chasing boys and dressing in the latest fashions. At fourteen, children should be happy with no worries or cares in the world. However, that was not the case for me, in fact, I felt sad most of the time. I had desperately wanted that kind of carefree life too. Unfortunately, my life was far more complex than that. I was doing my best to cover my sadness and the feelings of emptiness that had grown deep inside of me.

Happiness was something that always seemed just beyond my reach. The memories of being touched in all those very private places still haunted me. That was the reason that many nights, I lay awake in bed and cried myself to sleep. I would remember the tobacco smell on John's breath when he kissed me and the dampness of his palms when he touched me in all those forbidden places. I knew the memories would continue to haunt me; like deep scars, not even time could heal them.

Even as an adult, I still wonder how things would have turned out if I had told my parents that I had been molested those summers while in Philly. Would that have saved me from the horror I experienced with John? Since sexual abuse was not a topic that was openly discussed during my childhood years, unfortunately, I'll never know.

Chapter Eight

The Myth of Marriage

"Chains do not hold a marriage together. It is threads, hundreds of tiny threads which sew people together through the years." — Simone Signoret

As a little girl, I believed that when I got married and had a family, it would lead to a happy, fulfilling life. In real life, unfortunately, this belief proved itself wrong in a big way.

I met Rick shortly after my eighteenth birthday. From his irresistible personality, great sense of humor, beautiful green eyes and perfectly chiseled body, I thought that he was the answer to my prayers. The fact that he played basketball well enough to have earned a reputation throughout New Jersey made me adore him even more. What I found most attractive about him was his dedication to working with kids in schools and camps. Rick didn't take his talent for granted; he used his phenomenal athletic ability to help kids develop their potential to be the best they could be when it came to sports.

Neither Rick, nor I, could deny our strong, instant connection. There was a profound awareness of each other that happened just a few short moments after the first time we met. We met each other at Rick's house one night. It was a chance meeting, as I had gone there to visit his brother Elliot, but it was Rick, who answered the door instead. As it turned out, Elliot was not home, but Rick introduced himself as his older brother.

I was about to turn away and leave when Rick struck up a conversation, and we ended up talking for three hours that night. I enjoyed our conversation so much that I did not realize how quickly time flew by. Speaking to him made me feel like I had known him all my life. His friendly personality made me instantly feel comfortable with him. After getting to know him better, I realized that I loved everything about him, especially when he would tell corny jokes to cheer me up when I was having a bad day. He also had a way of making me feel special when he would lean his tall framed body down and kiss my forehead; he was so gentle and affectionate in that way. It didn't take long before we were inseparable. I couldn't wait to spend every single day with him. I loved how protective he was over me; he had a way of making me feel safe. That was the reason I felt I could never get enough of him.

I began to think of him as my knight in shining armor, enough so that I trusted him with my deepest, most shameful secret—my sexual molestation. Although he didn't receive the information as well as I had hoped he would, he did assure me that no matter what had happened to me in the past, he would never love me any less. That assurance helped me feel less like an outcast and more like a person.

I was thrilled that over the next few months, his fun-loving personality gradually began to tear down the walls of my rage. Slowly, but surely, Rick made me feel at ease. I could truly be myself with him, and the miracle was that in doing so, he still adored me.

I will always remember the day when we walked to the Union Flea Market holding each other close on a chilly winter evening, singing *Lionel Ritchie's* song, *You Are.* I felt the warmth of his love as he wrapped me in his arms, and I know he felt my love as well while I snuggled closer to his chest. That night will always be a very special memory for me. Our relationship was as close to perfect as any relationship could be, but it also had its ups and downs. Rick struggled with the fact that Elliot and I had a close friendship that started before Rick and I had gotten involved. He seemed extremely jealous when ironically, if it had not been for Elliot, Rick and I would have never met. However, Rick seemed to have a hard time letting go of the friendship Elliot and I still shared. I could see the jealousy in his eyes even as he continued to assure me he loved me. Soon it got hard to ignore the turbulence that was always there between us, hidden just beneath the surface.

We began to break up, and then get back together, repeatedly. It was during one of those break-ups that I found out I was pregnant with Rick's child. I will never forget the hot summer day when my doctor told me the test was positive—my pregnancy was a sure thing. The news caught me so off guard that I walked three miles home in the blistering heat, unable to put even a single coherent thought together except one—*what would my parents say?*

At the age of twenty, I knew for certain that my parents would definitely not approve. There would be no excitement or joy from them, that, I knew for sure. My next thoughts were even worse—I knew I had to tell Rick what was going on so that we could figure out we were going to do concerning the pregnancy.

I called him the next day, and we met that afternoon to discuss the pregnancy and make some plans. We decided to do the right thing for our baby, and get married. Back then, that is what people did when there was an unplanned pregnancy. I still held on to the marriage-and-family myth, although I already knew better. I found myself thinking only positive thoughts about my future and the shotgun future Rick and I faced together. I was in a wonderful space, at that point, a space in which it didn't matter what anyone else thought. I couldn't wait to have my baby.

We quickly arranged a small wedding and were married two weeks later, which was a huge surprise to both our families. It was no surprise to me when my parents didn't take the news or the prospect of the wedding too well. Nevertheless, in spite of their valid concerns, our wedding ceremony and the small celebration afterwards took place in the basement of my parents' home.

I expected the best—a happy marriage and a wonderful home for me and our baby on the way—as I took my vows while Rick slipped a ring on my finger. Surely, having a husband and a family would be enough to erase the painful memories that continued to haunt me; or at least I thought.

We moved into Rick's parent's basement for several months while we saved enough money to lease our own apartment. Seven months later, I gave birth to a perfect, beautiful seven pound, seven ounce baby girl. She was the most amazing sight I had ever seen. I was even more thrilled when I saw the way Rick looked at her, as if she was truly God's miracle.

We felt like the proudest parents in the world that year. All our relationship problems seemed to vanish in the midst of our child's birth. The joy of bringing a new life into the world convinced us that our future would be nothing but perfect. Every day was an amazing adventure and our beautiful daughter Shahnta, enriched our lives profoundly as we watched her grow and thrive.

Unfortunately, the good times lasted less than a year before Rick's behavior began to change. As busy as the baby kept me, I could still see that he was preoccupied with something other than me and Shahnta. He was getting home later and later each night for one thing. *Had he found another woman? Was he having an affair?* The thought would not leave my mind. I had to know the truth. I spent a couple of days building up my courage before I finally confronted him one night. I was even more shocked when the answer he gave was not that there was another woman in his life, but that he had been out smoking crack cocaine with a co-worker every night. He didn't lie, or try to hide his drug use; he just told me matter-of-factly where he had been and what he had been doing.

I had feared my husband was involved with another woman, but the truth was far worse; I knew crack cocaine was extremely more addictive than any personal relationship could ever be.

Crack had swept the nation in 1986 when it first came on the scene. Addicts would do anything and everything; even steal from their own parents to get the money they needed for another hit. That's how addictive the drug was.

The first time Rick offered crack to me, he sat on the couch in our dimly lit living room holding a glass, genie-shaped pipe in his hands. I hadn't seen anything like it in person before, and I watched as he pulled smoke from the stem that stuck out of the glass pipe. I cursed at him when he offered it to me. My only knowledge of crack was the fact that *Richard Pryor's* face had caught on fire while free-basing cocaine. Seeing the images of Mr. Pryor's burn injuries all over the newspapers and TV and hearing the stories about how addicted he was scared me enough not to try crack.

Not that I had never done cocaine before—far from it. At the time, I was no saint when it came to the occasional snorting of cocaine, and I was fine with snorting it the way I always had. Rick felt that he and I were a team. So since he had discovered this phenomenal drug, he didn't want me to miss out on the euphoria of what taking that first hit would feel like. Mistakenly viewing his willingness to share crack with me as a means of holding our marriage together; it wasn't long before temptation got the best of me. I finally agreed and gave it a try.

My husband was absorbed in the process of assembling the pipe carefully that night. He made sure every piece was put together as securely and perfectly as possible for my first hit. It was as if he was working on a major science project.

"I know this is taking a while, but it'll be worth it. You'll see," he told me repeatedly, as he continued working on his project.

When it was ready, he showed me how to pull on the stem at the same time he lit the small rocks with a makeshift cotton swab. The cotton was twisted on to a wire hanger, dipped in 151-proof rum to keep the fire lit.

I inhaled deeply on the pipe that night, taking all the smoke into my lungs. Within seconds, I was totally wrapped up in the feeling that I was floating on a gigantic pillow of clouds, a feeling that mesmerized me completely. Unfortunately, it lasted only about a minute—over with way too soon for my taste. At that point, I wanted to feel it again. I had to feel it again.

I didn't know then that no matter how many hits you take, after that first one, you never can recapture the feeling from that first hit. Every hit afterwards is a selfish attempt at getting that feeling over again. Each rock is a false promise of giving you that same high.

Those little white rocks turned out to be the beginning of the end of our marriage.

The crack took control of our lives quickly, turning us against each other. The fact that we spent all of our money on our addiction soon resulted in the fact that we could no longer pay our rent, buy groceries or pay our bills. We were high so much, that it resulted in our parents taking care of our little girl most of the time. It came as no surprise when we ended up separating later that year. We both believed that going our separate ways would help us address and deal with our addictions.

When I moved back to my parents' house, I was happy for the prospect of being able to stop smoking crack on my own. Rick, on the other hand, felt that he needed to go into rehab. I continued to support him as he completed his program; we then decided to move to California with one of his best friends. We believed, at that point, if we removed ourselves from the people, places and things that enabled us to use crack, somehow it would remove the addiction from our lives. What we didn't realize then was that we were the people, places and things that were causing us to use—and we were taking ourselves with us. It didn't take long for us to be back up to our old ways. We started smoking crack again just a few months after the move. Our new drug routine was ten times worse than before. We had no family out there or anyone to lean on to see the way we were ruining our lives.

It wasn't long before we sent our daughter back to New Jersey with our families so that we could check ourselves into rehab—my first rehab experience. I prayed to God that by going to rehab, I would be able to shake my addiction and finally have a normal life. With God's grace and support, I cleaned up my act and began attending twelve-step meetings faithfully and got a sponsor, as suggested by the rehab facility. At that point, my relationship with God had gotten stronger. I knew God loved me because He turned my life around. This motivated me to find a new way of life, one that could keep me clean. Getting clean was more of a struggle for Rick, but he was eventually able to get his life together too. I was clean but still not thinking clearly and decided that having another child would make all of our problems disappear. Needless to say, it didn't work.

WITHOUT PERMISSION

I was seven months pregnant when my husband was arrested on a drug-related charge. I went to court every day during his trial. My heart sank when the jury delivered a guilty verdict as I listened to the judge sentence Rick to two years in prison. I was devastated and felt Rick's addiction to crack cocaine destroyed our family. I couldn't hold back the tears. I'll never forget the weak, powerless feeling I got as the judge's voice echoed in my head.

It was at that point that I began to swing from sadness to fury, with Rick. How could he allow drugs to take him away from me? I loved him with all of my heart, which was the reason that the situation quickly became too much for me to bear.

Rick had been designated to serve out his term in a prison in Tracy, California, near San Francisco, a three-hour drive from our home in Los Angeles County. To make matters worse, the doctor had put me on bed rest so that my heavy bleeding would not result in a miscarriage.

One night while lying in bed, I could not stop crying. I felt totally alone and abandoned. It would be a long, long time before I saw Rick again. The reality of that fact consumed me. Looking back, I believe the stress of dealing with Rick's drug addiction and his resulting jail sentence all contributed to the complications in my pregnancy. It didn't help when later I had to find the drug dealer to whom Rick had sold our car to in exchange for drugs, to ask him if I could buy it back. I knew the drama was wearing me down, but I didn't realize how much it hurt me, not until I looked back on it years later.

I did make one important decision during that time—I made up my mind to move back to New Jersey. That way I could be closer to my family. My family would be a solid support system that my daughter, the new baby and I could all count on. I packed the apartment slowly and carefully, so as not to start up the bleeding again. Then I shipped everything I could back to New Jersey. I had to be strong for my daughter and my unborn child; there was no time for me to fall apart. The only way I could move on with my life was to leave my hurt and disappointments behind in California. That's what I kept telling myself and was what kept me going.

I went into premature labor about ten days after I got back to New Jersey. My doctor admitted me to the hospital and gave me medication to try and stop my labor pains. It didn't work. On a morning just a few days before Christmas, I gave birth to a beautiful baby girl that I named Amber. She was a healthy three pound-fifteen ounce premature baby. The joy that I felt washed away the sadness of Rick not being there to share the happy moment.

It was sad for me to go home without my new baby. She was kept on the neonatal ward in an incubator until she gained more weight. Amber was the smallest baby I had ever seen until I saw some of the other babies on the ward. Some of them weighed only 1 pound and were fiercely fighting for their lives. I was fearful of losing Amber and prayed to God that she was going to make it. She was my miracle baby, and I loved her with all of my heart. I made it a point each day to go to the hospital to bond with her, so she would know that her mother was there. I never missed a day out of the thirty days Amber stayed in the hospital. The day I took her home was one of the happiest days of my life.

By the time Amber had turned six months, she had gained a significant amount of weight and showed no signs of prematurity. Rick's mother, Amber and I flew to California so that Rick could finally meet his new daughter. The prison staff set up lodging for us during our visit, and allowed us to stay with him for a few days. It was difficult being in a prison setting with my child, but it was also a blessing to see her in Rick's arms. I remember thinking at the time that I hoped the whole trip would not be something that became a routine. I did not want my children getting use to seeing their father in jail.

I remained supportive of Rick while he did his time in jail, after all, he was my husband—the father of my children. So, I made sure he knew I was behind him, even if he was in jail. It was rough, but I kept the lines of communication open and gave him encouragement of eventually having a life on the outside of prison walls. Finally, due to good behavior, Rick received a parole transfer in 1992 and came home to his family in New Jersey. Once he was on the outside, we tried hard to make our life as a family work. Unfortunately, our efforts to make our marriage work proved impossible. Once outside the prison, Rick's desire to get high was in full force just like it had been before he went inside the concrete walls of the jail. Our desires to make the marriage work were not strong enough to overcome the reality that his drug addiction was still in the way.

I eventually had to surrender and let go of the marriage because I knew there was nothing more to be done to change things. The time we spent apart while he was in jail had put a wedge between us, and even though we thought we could start off right where things had ended when he went in, we couldn't.

We have both moved on with our lives and now are different people. I am grateful we remain friends to this day and have put the bad times and unhappy memories behind us.

Chapter Nine

Broken Pieces

"Love is like a puzzle. When you're in love, all the pieces fit but when your heart gets broken, it takes a while to get everything back together." — Author Unknown

I met Matthew a few months after Rick and I had separated. Matthew was a conductor on the New York/New Jersey train line I took to work each day. I was rushing to catch an early train home when I noticed him on the platform. At six feet, three inches tall, he towered over me and had smooth caramel-colored skin and beautiful diamond shaped eyes, which added to his already impressive stature.

His eyes could send me right into a trance—I knew that instantly somehow, but I didn't know then that the feeling would really come to pass. There I was, a newly single parent doing my best to adjust to my new and very stressful situation; just trying to survive. It was no wonder it had taken me a few months to notice Matthew. I had been in so much turmoil over the separation from Rick; I hadn't even taken the time to notice, much less look at another man.

That day, after the train doors shut, Matthew glided gracefully down the aisle while collecting tickets. He looked at me straight in my eyes when he reached my seat. He then lightly brushed my hand with his fingers as he took my ticket. I felt an instant shock run from my hand right through the rest of my body. The tingling sensation lingered and silenced me; I wasn't able to speak a word. The attraction was so strong and unexpected, that I felt mesmerized.

WITHOUT PERMISSION

From that moment on, I made a point of catching Matthew's train every day. I was determined to get to know him at all cost, even if I had to go out of my way just so I could be on his train. My wish to meet him finally came true in a very romantic way. One day, Matthew collected my train ticket, and then dropped a handful of coins on the floor right next to my seat. As he knelt down to pick them up, he looked straight into my eyes with a long, seductive stare. I felt his energy surround me, and then cut right through me. I felt like melting in my seat, just from his glance. Matthew and I exchanged phone numbers before I got off the train, and after that, we began to talk on the phone regularly.

Matthew later admitted that he had deliberately dropped the coins in front of me. I was pleasantly surprised and also as flattered as I had ever been in my life. No man had done anything like that to catch my attention. I knew the relationship was going to be serious, as soon as we started dating, a few weeks later. Our connection was just as intense as our first encounter. It was obvious to me that although my marriage had wounded me deeply; somehow with Matthew in my life, I was ready to move on with my future.

It was easy to fall in love with Matthew when his top priority was taking care of me and my daughters. I also admired his excellent work ethic—he was determined to get ahead in the world. I loved it when he would show up at my house with bags full of groceries and then cook a delicious dinner that we always enjoyed. Irresistibly handsome, ambitious, a good cook and a man who cared deeply for me and my girls—it didn't get much better than that in my book.

It didn't take long before I suggested we move in together. As close as we had become, I knew Matthew would complete me as well as my family. I was thrilled when he turned out to be as happy with that idea as I was. We found a bigger apartment located on a quiet cult-de-sack not far from where I was living and furnished it together. We created a warm and cozy home that reflected both our personalities.

I truly believed Matthew would give me the family life I had always longed for. I wanted to feel secure and felt he could provide that for me.

He had worked with the railroad for a very long time, owned a restaurant and was attentive to me and my daughters. We complimented each other so nicely, I couldn't help but to believe we were truly a perfect couple.

Things were great when we moved in together. I was particularly happy when Matthew planted a beautiful flower garden in our front yard. He told me he did it for me. His wonderful qualities never ceased to surprise me—Matthew was the perfect man. I wanted to marry him, but I knew that couldn't happen until I closed the final chapter with Rick. I found out how to file for a divorce and began the process. I planted all the seeds. I just had to wait and make sure I was ready when Matthew decided to ask me to marry him!

One beautiful summer Sunday afternoon, Matthew, my daughters and I were picnicking up at South Mountain Reservation. We were having a great time until Matthew's cell phone rang. His father had fallen ill and had been rushed to the hospital. We packed up and left quickly; Matthew needed to be with his father, and we were the loving family that would be by his side.

When he finally got home late that night from the hospital, he was sad and upset. He told me that he needed to talk to me, but this time, he couldn't look me in my eye. My heart sank as he told me how lucky he felt that his father was in stable condition, and then he sprung it on me that his family needed him back home to help run the family church.

Matthew's father was a Bishop, who had started the church when Matthew and his siblings were young. Matthew had grown up in the church, and had become a Pastor under his father's supervision. He looked at me sadly because he had a choice to make that night. It was either the church and his birth family or me and the girls.

His family had made no secret of the fact that they disapproved of our living together, nor were his parents, particularly fond of me in general. One Thanksgiving, when Matthew brought me and the girls to his parents' house for dinner, his father told us clearly how unhappy he was with our living arrangements. I left his parents' home that night feeling disappointed and rejected. While it was true that Matthew and I were not married, I believed it was just a matter of time before he would ask me to marry him and make everything right.

Unfortunately, it was never going to be. Matthew debated the decision that had been forced on him for several weeks, which caused a lot of stress between us; stress that resulted in an increasing number of arguments between us, some of which escalated into physical fights. At that point, the connection we had both felt, began to slowly unravel. We soon reached an important realization that our relationship would never work. Matthew made the painful decision of moving out after our final, and particularly intense, fight. It was then that I knew for sure, that my dreams of a happily ever after relationship with Matthew were not meant to be.

I had been clean from cocaine for several years when I met Matthew, although I smoked marijuana occasionally, along with some social drinking while we were together. I felt okay with that, until Matthew, and I started having knocked down, drag out, fights. The stress, discomfort and sadness soon caused me to leave the apartment and go out to do the same thing I always did to comfort myself—I snorted cocaine.

I had shared my battle with cocaine addiction and my hidden secrets with Matthew early in our relationship. What I loved about him was that he never judged me. As our relationship came to a bitter end, I couldn't bear to tell him that my cocaine use had become as frequent as the fights we were having.

I was devastated when he left; broken-hearted from yet another failed relationship. In addition to the loneliness of not having Matthew by my side, I was clueless as to how the girls and I were going to make it financially. Although I had a great job at the pharmaceutical company, my salary would simply not cover the comfortable lifestyle I had become accustomed to with Matthew's income as a bonus. My mother knew a young lady who made fairly good money from her paper route, and she suggested I get one of my own. I was determined not to let my ship sink and decided to give it a try.

I applied for a newspaper carrier position with one of the largest newspapers in our area. I felt lucky to land that part-time job even though

I knew I would have to get up at 3:00 AM and deliver more than 200 papers within a few hours. I knew it would be a challenge, but I felt ready for it. I needed to do it, if my girls and I were going to make it. One good thing was that I had access to the garage in my house and there was a table already set up where I could sort and assemble all the papers before heading out the door.

I'll never forget my first day on the job. I brought home heavy bundles of papers to prepare for Sunday, which was the biggest delivery day of the week. I hauled everything into the garage, looked at the papers and began to cry. *How would I get all these stacks of papers organized and assembled?* I thought to myself feeling overwhelmed. It was a huge challenge, and I was grateful my mother was visiting that day and was more than willing to offer her help. With her assistance, I soon got the hang of it, and completed everything more quickly than I would have ever believed I could.

I was a delivery pro within a few weeks' time, and soon found out my mother was right—the salary plus tips did help me meet my expenses. I was extremely relieved to know I could make it on my own.

Even though the new job was working out well financially; my heart still ached because Matthew was gone. I missed him terribly and cried every night. Our relationship had ended so abruptly it broke my heart, and I hadn't had time to heal. Although we continued to see each other periodically, I knew we would never be a family again. I began to snort cocaine more and more often. Then, it was just a matter of time before I got the urge for something stronger—crack cocaine.

It had been years since Rick, and I divorced to only be in the same place again. I just didn't want to feel the pain anymore. The lonelier and more depressed I felt, the more crack I smoked. The addiction had gotten the best of me again. My nights were filled with meeting my suppliers alone in seedy alleyways and abandoned buildings. I didn't care about the possibilities of the hidden danger. My main priority was to score. Looking back, I know now that it was only God's grace that prevented me from getting raped or murdered.

WITHOUT PERMISSION

My pain was so monumental that I felt like I could barely think at all. Emotionally, I wasn't there for my girls. I was leaving Shahnta to baby sit her sister every night, while I ran off to feed my addiction. Being a mother was low on the totem pole compared to the need to feed my addiction.

I couldn't wait until the end of the workday to hurry off and speed down Route 78 to Newark where I bought my drugs. I never took the time to change out of my business clothes either, which made me stand out like a sore thumb. Nor did I think about the possible consequences of my actions while buying crack. I never thought I could have been a victim of a violent attack or arrested for drug possession. I would have most likely lost my children, a possibility that never crossed my mind at the time.

One evening, while I was on my way to get high at a crack house in Newark, I found myself caught in the middle of a shoot-out. The fact that my only concern was how to get from my car to the crack house without being shot shows how totally out of touch I was with reality. Addiction was my jailer at that point. I truly, deeply believed I needed crack cocaine to survive, and unfortunately, put my life in jeopardy to get it. I hated myself for what I had become; but I didn't have the will to surrender and let it go.

If I had no idea that God was protecting me at the time, I know now that He most definitely made the difference between life and death for me back in those days.

That night, after the shootout, I found a dealer who promised he could sell me some drugs. I felt a little uneasy about buying from someone I really didn't know, but I wasn't willing to deny myself the substance I needed so badly without having to go back to the place where I normally scored.

I was totally unprepared when some unmarked police cars pulled up and surrounded my car just as the dealer and I were about to close the transaction. An undercover police officer ran to the passenger side and pulled the dealer out of my car while a second officer ordered me to hand over my keys and driver's license. I made up a story very quickly as he began to question me. I told the officer that I was there to pick up my cousin from her friend's house but wasn't sure which apartment her friend lived in. Then I saw this gentleman standing by the building. I had no idea he was a drug dealer when I asked him if he knew my cousin's friend. He said he knew her but didn't know what apartment she lived in and needed to use my cell phone in order to find out, which was the reason he was sitting in my car when the officer showed up.

I eased the money from my hand, as I told the tale, and slid it into my coat pocket. I knew God was with me when the officer handed back my keys and license, told me I didn't belong in Newark and added it would be best to go home and never come back to that part of town.

A normal person would have been thrilled to be let off the hook so easily. However, thanks to my drug use, I was far from normal that night. Instead of heading home as the officer had so strongly suggested, I drove down the street to another crack house and asked someone else to purchase it for me. I was willing to risk everything to get my drugs and block out the pain. Even my close brush with the law couldn't deter me from that goal.

Drugs were the only way I had ever known to comfort myself, and I hated myself for it. I felt abandoned—again—when Matthew left me, and I continued to get high to block the pain of his rejection. Even though I knew how quickly the drugs could destroy my life or even kill me.

My need for drug money was so strong, that even though it was hard on me physically, I continued to wake up and deliver newspapers in the middle of the night. I would come home, get my girls ready for school and grab about an hour of sleep before it was time to go to my full-time job. Looking back, it's hard for me to believe I could do it.

My mother and sister soon sensed something was terribly wrong with me, and they came up from North Carolina to check everything out. As much as I tried to hide my addiction, I had no choice but to come clean with them. When they suggested they would take my girls to live with them in North Carolina until I could get my life back together, I agreed.

Having to part with my girls was painful. Because my life was in a downward spiral, I could no longer care for them the way they needed to be cared for. I also knew that if my family had not intervened, it was just a matter of time before social services took my daughters away from me permanently.

The arrangement my mother and sister suggested was temporary, but the reality of it hit me hard. I knew that I had to get clean, if not for myself, then for my daughters.

Chapter Ten

Planting the Seed of Faith

"Now faith is the substance of things hoped for, the evidence of things not seen." — Hebrews 11:1

Of all the possible consequences of my cocaine addiction, losing my children was the worst. It was a possibility that never failed to cause my chest to tighten and give me a dark, empty feeling in the pit of my stomach. Even though that possibility haunted me, it wasn't enough to bring me to the point where I was willing to stop getting high right away.

It hurt me deeply when my mother and sister took my children back with them to North Carolina. I knew it would be an abrupt and painful interruption in their young lives. It's always a hard transition for children to be uprooted from their home and their friends. Even worse, I knew that it was all entirely my fault. I found myself living in a personal hell at that point. I realized I needed to go back to rehab if I ever planned to get them back. I knew, suddenly, that only God could save me; I could never do it on my own.

Even though I wasn't sure what to do next, God took over and started the process for me. I fell into a deep depression about a week before my 35th birthday and knew I needed professional help. I found a local psychiatrist in Summit, New Jersey, who was willing to see me right away. My hope was that he'd give me some kind of quick fix to take away all the pain I was feeling.

WITHOUT PERMISSION

The doctor suggested that I take a leave of absence from my job at the pharmaceutical company in order to give myself time for the anti-depressants he was prescribing to work. I was happy at first when he prescribed not one, but three, separate anti-depressants with instructions for me to take them together. He then added a fourth to provide immediate relief. It was a drug usually prescribed for psychosis and/or schizophrenia.

At the time, I was happy to have some relief from the pain, and I secretly expected the medications to lift me out of the pit I was living in, but I soon found out that I was in for a surprise. The drugs made me feel lethargic to the point of not being able to function normally. Taking a shower in the morning and getting dressed required the effort of Hercules. I couldn't drive my car either, because I felt drowsy all the time, and it was not unusual for me to stay in bed all day.

During that time, my daughters were having a hard time adjusting to life in North Carolina, and I hadn't heard from Matthew in weeks. I was a mental and physical mess. I shook uncontrollably and had cold sweats as I lay in bed all day. I also couldn't sleep at night, and all I did was toss and turn, unable to settle down.

I found out later that I was experiencing all the worst side effects of the antidepressants. I felt like I was in a new and different personal hell. I listened to the eerie silence around me as I felt the walls closing in on me. Even the air seemed to suffocate to me.

Sadness engulfed me as I remembered how just a few months earlier my house had been filled with joy and laughter. I rocked back and forth in my bed crying uncontrollably. I was upset with myself for the direction my life was taking. In the midst of my thoughts, the telephone rang. I looked at the caller ID before I picked it up—it was my cousin Ferrell, a pastor in Georgia, who called to check in with me every so often.

He knew about my battle with drugs. He also knew my family had taken temporary custody of my girls. I had told him how Matthew and I had broken up too and how I felt like I was in the worst shape of my life. I hoped Ferrell would have something constructive to say as I took his call.

He first suggested we pray together, something we always did, whenever he called me. That day, the prayer was different. He seemed to sense how devastated I was, and he suggested I read a Bible scripture; Hebrews 11:1; "*Now faith is the substance of things hoped for, the evidence of things not seen.*" Ferrell urged me to read it daily, and he assured me that if I put my trust in God, my life would get better. I was in so much pain and desperate for anything that might give me any hope at all that I followed his instructions to the letter.

Reading the scripture didn't work, at least not right away. When I woke up on my 35th birthday, I felt like I no longer wanted to live. It was a gloomy day in March, with patches of winter snow still on the ground. The sun was nowhere in sight, nor were there any visible signs that spring would ever come. I felt drugged, hopeless and almost lifeless from the antidepressants. I had no will to live.

It's hopeless! That's what I told myself that morning. *I need to end it all right now.* The thoughts were chanting over and over in my head. Suicide was suddenly a viable choice. I picked up a bottle of *Tylenol 3*, the one with Codeine in it, and I held the bottle tightly in my hands.

*I'll take the whole bottle; take all the pills right now...*the suicidal chanting began again.

I began to open the bottle until I realized I couldn't kill myself without saying good-bye to my girls. *A note—I'll write them a note!* I shouted out loud through tears, which were streaming down my face as I went to get some paper and a pen. I sat down, then holding the pen in one hand and the bottle of pills in the other; I tried to gather my thoughts through my drug haze. I put the bottle down and began the good-bye letter to my daughters:

My beloved daughters:
I want to tell you both how sorry I am for failing you as a mother. I love you both with all of my heart, and I am sorrier than words can ever say that I can't be here for you right now...

I looked at the words, and knew that I couldn't keep going. It was better to end it all right then. I took a deep breath for courage, and suddenly, a voice inside of me said, *Hold on. Hold on just a little longer...*

Then I remembered Fair Oaks, a private psychiatric hospital and treatment center in Summit, New Jersey, which specialized in drug and alcohol addiction. *If only they will admit me and let me stay there a few days, maybe I won't hurt myself.* My mind was still trying to rationalize my situation. As much as I felt like I wanted to die, I couldn't ignore the voice of God. He told me there was hope and urged me to keep going.

I forced myself to look up the hospital's number and make the call. The woman who answered spoke softly and sounded nice, that helped me continue taking the steps I needed to in order to survive. When she asked me my name, I told her, and I also informed her of my plans to end my life by swallowing the bottle of pills. She listened closely and then told me how Fair Oaks could help me.

She continued questioning me in a very caring manner. I found myself laying the bottle of pills down and willingly answering her questions. I told her about my cocaine addiction, and then she asked for my medical insurance information. After twenty minutes on the phone, she told me there was a bed available. I could have it, if I got there ASAP. I agreed to do so. After all, I knew my life depended on it.

I felt a bit of relief and was hopeful that I would finally get the help I needed. I quickly threw some clothes in a bag and jumped in my car. I pulled up in front of an old, brown brick building twenty five minutes later. I parked my car and hurried inside. Instantly, I felt a little better when an older woman with silver hair and a warm smile greeted me. When I gave her my name, she said they were expecting me.

She directed me to the intake office where the nurse I'd spoken to on the phone greeted me. She asked me to have a seat, and then asked for the bottle of pills I had planned to take. When I handed her the bottle, she assured me I was in the right place. Her demeanor and the gentle seriousness of her words made me believe that Fair Oaks would provide me with a safe environment where I could heal.

After a lengthy admission process, the nurse took me to the cafeteria to meet the other patients. To my surprise, the patients and staff began to sing *Happy Birthday,* and then presented me with a beautiful birthday cake. Celebrating a landmark birthday, my 35th, on a psychiatric ward was a bittersweet moment for me. It was not quite what I had in mind for a celebration. However, I felt a moment of clarity as I realized that I was still alive only a couple of hours after wanting to kill myself. The birthday celebration made me feel better, for a little while.

Even after all the trouble I found myself in and how bleak life had seemed, I found some gratitude. God could and would save me, and I believed that with all my heart. I was even more thankful when I reached the realization that He, if no one else, believed I was still worth saving.

After my birthday celebration, someone took me up to my room. I expected a private room with a nurse to look after me. I was surprised to see that I was sharing a room with another patient who had also attempted suicide. I was equally surprised when the nurse informed me that I was on the psychiatric ward. I knew I had suicidal thoughts, but it never occurred to me that I needed psychiatric care.

I had secretly hoped and prayed that I would be sedated until my pain subsided. That didn't happen either. Later, I realized that I was integrated with other patients on the ward, who had serious psychiatric issues. The next evening, I was allowed visitation. Two of my closest friends came to offer encouragement, and confirmed that I didn't belong on a psychiatric ward.

I was glad to hear them say that because the psychiatric ward terrified me. Especially, since I'd never been on one before. There was a patient there who kept punching the walls until his knuckles bled. He was restrained in a strait jacket for his own protection. To make matters worse, I couldn't sleep because there was another patient who screamed all night for no apparent reason. It took just one day for me to realize that I was not in a facility that could help me heal. To be quite honest, being there made my pain deeper by association.

By the grace of God, I still had my sanity, and I proceeded to check myself out the next day. I was informed by the ward nurse that there was a 72-hour clause on the admittance sheet that I had signed. I had only been there almost 48 hours at that point, not long, but long enough for me to take a good look at my life from a different point of view. It was also enough time to jolt me into reality and remind me how far I had really come on my life journey.

I realized right then and there, that if I could somehow manage to cling to just a little hope, it might be possible for me to turn my life around. I thought back to what my cousin Ferrell suggested about reading the Hebrews' scripture in the Bible. I decided to try faith, the strongest faith I'd ever possessed, to turn my life around.

Fair Oaks allowed me to sign myself out the next evening. By that time, I had a brand-new outlook and a much greater appreciation for my life. I hadn't spent much time there, but I felt like I was back in the real world, free to live my life and turn it around if I tried hard enough.

I thought back to the patients on the ward and how many of them had no choices. I deeply appreciated the choices I knew I was lucky enough to have. How wonderful it felt to know I was on my way home.

My Fair Oaks experience had been valuable in giving me a whole new perspective on my life, and willingness to put my trust in God. The opportunity to do that presented itself quickly when someone suggested that I attend a revival at Fountain Baptist, a local church in Summit. Ironically, it wasn't far from Fair Oaks.

I was pleasantly surprised when I attended the revival. The hope and spirit that surrounded me allowed me to go home feeling much better about my life. On the third day of the revival, a young pastor gave a testimony about how he had turned his life over to Christ. His sermon filled me with so much hope that I knew that I, too, was ready to turn my life over to Christ. All that I had been through had given me the chance to see how God pulled me through some trying times and destructive behavior. It was His love that kept me. I knew that my decision to turn my will and my life over to His care would be one of the best decisions I had ever made. I joined that church and quickly scheduled a date to be baptized.

As I began to walk with Christ, I came to the realization that you must love yourself before you can love anyone else. I had been so desperate to fill the spiritual void inside of me. I tried to heal the wound instantly, by putting a band-aid on it. That was easier than having to do the work necessary to heal the old internal wounds. At the same time, I had a need for someone else to love me because I didn't know how to love myself. I looked for love in every relationship and then wondered why they never worked out. My repeated attempts at putting a band-aid over a gaping wound was unsuccessful. God had to get my attention in order for me to trust in Him and His powers. Facing storms, then being rescued by God, strengthened my faith immeasurably. God showed me, every day of my life, how He was there for me. Now, years later, I can clearly see how much He loves me rather than regarding the events of my life as coincidences, as I had in the past.

I know now that every life storm is an opportunity for us to practice our faith. How can we have a testimony if we don't first have a test? God is always working on something far greater and better for our lives than anything we can ever imagine. We must be patient and allow the miracles to unfold.

I now believe that God's plan for me is, and has always been, perfect. Unfortunately, I couldn't understand that plan and how it was going to work until I was thoroughly convinced the morning, I heard Him speak to me. There were tears of gratitude and joy that streamed down my face, as I prayed. I felt His presence in my room. Warmth suffused my body as He very clearly told me that He wanted me to minister to others. I giggled at first. I couldn't imagine myself ministering to anyone. I felt unworthy of such a calling.

How was God intending to use me? I asked myself.

I always believed in order to do God's work you had to be squeaky clean, almost perfect. However, that day, I found out that God also uses people who are far less than perfect to carry His message.

The Bible tells stories of people God has used, including Hannah *(1 Samuel 1:1-28, 1 Samuel 2:1-10, 1 Samuel 2:19, 1 Samuel 25:12).*

Hannah is described as a passionate woman who was deeply in tuned with God. She was shown as a true servant of the Lord, and always gave praise even though her womb was closed, and could not have children. Her story clearly shows that regardless of her obstacle, she never stopped praising God. God uses people we'd least expect to do His work and spread His message. Hannah displayed humility without bitterness. Thinking of her, reminded me that God is always faithful, even when we think we've been defeated. Through every obstacle that I have faced, I've learned to appreciate God's grace and mercy.

There are days when I am challenged by the demons of my past, and reality is, temptation will always be there. Even when those times attack me and test my faith, I still continue to praise God. I will not throw away the goodness that God has brought into my life. Having had moments of fear of being rejected and judged from telling my story has consumed me. However, God has confirmed and reassured me that He stands with me. It is the spirit of fear that keeps us in bondage. I refuse to be in bondage any longer. God has been preparing me all along. He has shown me that sharing my story and spreading the word of His goodness is my way of ministering. I know now that it is only God's grace, love and forgiveness that have saved me. I can never repay Him for where He has brought me today. This is why I spread the word about His love, grace and mercy.

As my spiritual and healing journey continues, many positive changes occur, in my life. These days, I walk with a confident stride, fully aware of my destination. I wear a smile on my face because my spirit and many of my burdens have been lifted. I am happy when people notice my outer glow, something that radiates from deep inside of me. I am walking in the light of God and know that He is always with me. Whatever troubles I face, I am confident that He will bring me through it. If He brings you to it, He will bring you through it. I no longer let my worries consume me because I trust in God's promises. Philippians 4:13, *"I can do all things through Christ, which strengthens me."* The possibilities in life are endless. I know God will truly see me and all of us through whatever challenges we face.

Chapter Eleven

Freedom Through Forgiving

"Forgiveness is the key to the gift of inner peace."
— *Sharon R. Wells*

The most important thing that I learned about forgiveness was that the first person I needed to forgive was me. Forgiving others is hard. It entails us stepping outside of our hurts and fears long enough to be Godlike in our behavior. That's hard to do, but if we have any sort of relationship with God, we find a way to own a spirit of forgiveness. Sometimes we do that with the caveat of, 'forgiving, but not forgetting.' Even if we choose not to forget, somehow, because of the influence of God, we find a way to forgive others.

However, it can be more difficult to extend that same spirit of forgiveness towards ourselves. We have a tendency to be harder on our own actions, or lack thereof, concerning the actions of others.

In my own circumstances, I realized that I was very angry at my abusers. I always found ways to make excuses for what they did to me by minimizing it. I fooled myself into thinking that I wasn't as hurt as I was. Only with the passage of time, and a deep glance at how I was carrying the anger around like a chip on my shoulder, was I able to lighten my emotional load. Once I did, I was able to forgive my attackers. That release did not include the blame I placed on myself. Somehow, I had forgiven them and shifted the blame to me.

While I thought that I was finding ways of getting over the pain and coping with the abuse, I still had not forgiven myself. I was simply putting makeup on the black eye of my heart, hoping like a battered wife, that no one would notice the bruise. It took a lot of therapy, but I finally realized how impossible it is to heal a heart that is filled with anger and bitterness; specifically, when those feelings are directed towards the acceptance of oneself. I held on to the anger and bitterness for such a long period of time. It kept me in mental and emotional bondage and attracted all kinds of negativity, like a moth to a flame, in every aspect of my life.

I was angry with myself and resentful concerning the sexual abuse for most of my life. It was an inner hatred that I could not shake for a very long time. Much more important, I truly and deeply believed that I had done something to cause the abuse to happen to me. I felt like I had a neon sign on my forehead that lit up as an advertisement requesting abusers to use me at will. I did not realize until I went through therapy that I was not responsible for what my abusers had done to me. Their sins were not mine to bear. There wasn't anything that I had said or did to warrant being used and abused. It was a long journey to get to that place of fruition and acceptance.

I found, along my journey of self-forgiveness, that many victims feel guilty and ashamed when abuse happens to them. They carry the guilt that something they did had to have been an instigator of their torment and pain. Victims fail to realize that predators don't need provocation, their need to prey on the weak and innocent is fuel enough.

If you are the victim of abuse the most important thing for you to remember is this: **it is not your fault!** You cannot and should not take ownership of someone else's actions. In committing the act of abuse, the perpetrator wanted to take your power. Don't continue to let them have it by owning their sins as your own. You must stop the cycle by reclaiming your power and forgiving yourself. Only then can you learn to nurture the wounded child inside of you, as I did.

Thinking back to my own abuse still hurts me. Only with the help of God have I been able to move forward beyond the abuse and beyond the pain. I continue to pray for my abusers, realizing that they need God's help just as much as I do, and I'm always careful not to wish them any harm. They are lost souls that need guidance, and the spirit of forgiveness has shown me not to desire vengeance for my pain.

At one point in my therapy, I decided to confront one of my abusers. I had to muster up the courage to tell him how negatively he had impacted my life. It was very therapeutic for me. I needed to step from behind my shame and put the blame where it belonged, in his lap. Although, I knew the confrontation wouldn't change the past and what had happened; it was very empowering and definitely helped me move forward in my healing process. Confronting my abuser was also an opportunity to dissipate some of the pain that resulted from the fact that I could not stand up for myself as a child. There was an extreme sense of gratification in that role reversal.

Forgiveness did not happen overnight, nothing lasting ever does. I knew it was something I wanted to work on, and something I needed for my own peace of mind. Healing was so important to me, and I knew I could not make any progress without a spirit of forgiveness. I relied strongly on God to give me that spirit. I trusted that if I could just begin to take care of myself with the faith of a mustard seed, He would do the rest.

I knew it was time to clear out and remove the anger and bitterness that were festering inside me. A feeling I like to compare to having high cholesterol. Cholesterol blocks our arteries, preventing blood from pumping freely to our hearts and through our bodies. Anger felt the same way to me; it kept me stuck and blocked me from growing and loving. My anger harmed me much more than the abusers whom I had convinced myself I would always hate. The lingering feeling hurt me more than the person had.

I also knew that part of my journey to healing included a need for me to forgive my parents. I had chosen to protect them from all the details of my abuse when it happened. As a teen, misguided in my feelings and not knowing where to turn, I was angry with them for not being able to see the signs that I had been abused. I was even angrier that they had not realized that my drug use and destructive behavior all stemmed from the abuse. I harbored a sense of resentment that they could not see past the walls I had built up. It was because I found a way to disguise the source of my pain. That feeling hung around my neck like an expensive silk tie of blame.

Later in life, as part of my therapy and healing process, I made the decision to talk to my parents about my trauma and my feelings towards them. It was a powerful step that helped us all to begin healing. The unspoken demon was finally slayed.

Most people don't recognize the fact that victims are not the only ones harmed by abuse. Many parents, who learn that their children have been abused, suffer a great deal of anger, emotional pain and guilt as well. Most of the time, the family, as a whole, suffers in shame. The abuse becomes a dirty little secret kept in the hall closet, out of the sight of others. Everyone involved feels that they are the cause or source of its conception. In fact, it is not uncommon for parents of abused children to beat themselves up emotionally for years. They feel they did not protect their child in a manner that would never have left them vulnerable to the abuse in the first place. Sometimes parents blame themselves more than the perpetrator, for what happened.

Sexual abuse overwhelms both the victim and his or her family with a tremendous sense of guilt and shame. The victim feels the physical trauma, and yet, that same trauma reaches out like branches on a tree to all those remotely connected to the victim. When confronted with sexual molestation, some families prefer to keep their problems inside of their homes. They falsely believe that outside help is not needed and family unity will be enough to ease and erase all pain. I now know that the whole family unit can benefit from professional counseling if they participate in it together. Once a family can articulate in their words and actions that the *unthinkable* has actually happened in *their* family, then and only then, can the bond of family unity conquer all. Counseling helps each member to heal and be freed from their own individual, self-imposed, guilt and shame.

Once I made the choice to go into therapy, the greatest reward I received, was the way it helped me find the courage to tell my parents how angry I was for so many years. My parents, in turn, shared their hurt and told me how much they suffered after they found out about the abuse. That cathartic exchange was priceless. Although geographic factors made it impossible for us physically to go to therapy together, breaking the silence by discussing the abuse helped us in many ways.

Having put the chore of forgiving my abuser, myself and my parents behind me, I had one more obstacle to tackle. The last, but rather critically important thing I had to face and forgive myself for, was the trauma, I had put my children through. They were the silent victims in the trickle-down effect of my abuse as a child. A generation distanced my girls from my past and my abuse, yet both affected them, as if they were cemented in their present and future. My failure to deal with my past spilled over into my ability to deal with them in any aspect, on more occasions than I am willing to admit. I had always prided myself on being a good mother, but at some point, I missed the mark. I have to admit that the two miracles of my life that should have had center stage in everything I did got put on the back burner to my self-destructive behavior.

I knew I had definitely failed my daughters at certain times in their lives. However, I also knew that in order to fully heal, I had to admit and address that fact. It was only through therapy, that I learned that the best I can do, is the best I can do. No one is perfect and we all fall short, including me. That's not an excuse on my part, it's a reality. Sometimes we have to remove the rose-colored glasses of denial and just accept things as they are or were, and take steps accordingly towards corrective action. I will never be able to get those years in my daughter's lives back. I can't erase the fact that I was not there for them at certain times in their lives when they needed me most. All I can do as an afterthought is recognize where I screwed up and follow a path that ensures that their lives are enriched with my presence from here going forward.

I am glad to say that I've also accepted the message from God of how forgiving children can be in nature. There is nothing more wonderful than the unconditional love for a parent given by a child. That message echoes from our love of our Heavenly Father to spilling over into our own personal relationships with our children. A child's love is unconditional and has no boundaries. For that I am truly grateful. My daughters love me, respect me, and are proud of me, despite all the mistakes I've made along the way. My mistakes and irresponsible choices made their lives harder than what it should have been. They never used it against me or as sources of ridicule or retaliation. Their pride and love are the best and the most rewarding gifts of all.

The gifts, in the form of my daughters' unconditional love and pride in me, were just what I needed in order to start looking at myself differently. I began giving myself the same unconditional love that I received from them. I began to feel inner peace and self-love as I explored the issues that resulted from my abuse. A trained therapist helped me to deflate the air in the balloon cycle of abuse that was my life and potentially theirs. My new feelings about myself became the helium to a new balloon of a life cycle for us all to follow. Their love helped us break a vicious cycle. We were able to start a new and build upon a foundation of understanding and persevering in spite of.

Like the healing process, my journey through forgiveness was slow and difficult. In the end, I was glad to find out that anything is possible when we ask God to soften our hearts and ask Him to give us the courage we need to move forward. He is the potter and we are the clay, but sometimes we have to ask Him to mold us. However, we must be willing to yield to Him in order for it to happen.

The lesson I learned during my journey to forgiveness was simple yet profound. I found out that only when we forgive others, as well as ourselves completely, then we are able to move on with our lives. It allows our hearts to receive all the blessings and love that God has waiting for us.

Chapter Twelve

Overcoming the Battle Within

*"The most important of life's battles is the one we fight
daily in the silent chambers of the soul."* — *David O. McKay*

It was very important for me during my healing process to find someone
I could trust and be totally honest with. I needed to feel safe before I
could open up and reveal all of my deepest and darkest secrets. It took
time to build a trusting relationship. In order to do so, I had to be patient
with myself and others in order to feel comfortable enough to open up
and reveal my past. I also had to be willing to revisit the painful memories
that I had blocked out for so very long. Surrendering and accepting my
feelings was challenging for me. Luckily, after a while, I found the right
therapist to help me. I felt very comfortable with Nan and knew that I
had finally found a therapist whom I could completely trust. Her warm
and caring personality made it easy for me to let down the walls I had
built up for years. I was able to tell her about every aspect of my sexual
molestation.

Before I began to work with Nan, I knew my drug addiction had
always gotten in the way, taking precedence over the real reason I went
to therapy. In terms of my relationships with therapists, I had used my
drug addiction and depression as a smoke screen. It allowed me to avoid
thoroughly facing my sexual molestation and the ways in which it had
damaged me.

Although I had gone into therapy several times, all voluntarily, I
wasn't really ready for therapy until I met Nan. The denial of my real

intentions with therapy was evidenced by the way I generally stopped going after the therapists urged me to talk about being molested.

The more I talked with Nan about the abuse and could accept my feelings, the easier therapy became. Healing is a very personal and unique experience; every person finds solace at his or her own individual pace. What may be beneficial for one person may not be the remedy for another. Therapy was very beneficial to me because it helped me look at life from a positive perspective and forced me to embrace forgiveness.

Even with all the time and effort spent working through my problems in therapy, I still wrestle with a void within my spirit. This uncomfortable feeling has found a resting place. Occasionally, and without notice, lonely, empty feelings come up to remind me that healing does not happen overnight. The voice of my pain is the reality of how deeply rooted the trauma is within me and how profoundly it has affected my life. It hurts when these sudden flashbacks of my sexual abuse suddenly and abruptly interrupt moments of peace, even joy and happiness, in my life.

There are times when I cry for the little girl inside me who is deeply saddened. I wonder why those horrible things had to happen to me. I can't help but reflect on how all of it has molded and shaped me into the woman I have become today. One part of the answer is simple; I have had to overcome much in my lifetime. I have found great strength through adversity. As I move into the future, I'm glad to know that as long as I keep my faith planted firmly in God, the painful feelings I experience will pass.

Healing from abuse is an ongoing process. Although I'm happy for my progress, I can't imagine that any victim ever fully recovers from the wounds. The scars resulting from sexual abuse are so deeply embedded within the spirit that it can take a lifetime to properly peel off the layers of damage that has been done.

I also believe God allows us to experience certain issues in our lives repeatedly, until we become ready to address them. We can't run from our demons; God wants us to address them and be triumphant over them. When God is satisfied that we've learned the lesson we were supposed to learn, He will then allow us to move forward.

I will continue my healing journey and share my story in an attempt to be an advocate for abuse victims everywhere. I have learned that no matter the nature and depth of the struggle, no matter how many lessons I need to learn, I can always count on God to do His work. I, like so many abuse victims, am a work in progress.

In my case, He continues to use me to uplift others. My life story of battling with drug addiction, failed relationships and depression is clearly a direct result of how God can turn things around. From the pits of being in crack houses and losing my children to being an advocate for victims everywhere, God uses me. He keeps me strong during the times when I am weak. Whenever I am in a place where I can't help myself, He sends someone to help me. That continued open-arm of love extends to me each day. No matter how low I get in my feelings or in my actions, He is always there for me. He loves His children no matter what they do.

A dear friend shared with me that even in the midst of spiritual warfare; God gives us His gifts unconditionally. I was feeling really bad about myself, and I wanted to give up on everything, so I prayed. A friend happened to show up and reminded me that regardless of the things we do, it doesn't take away the gifts that God has blessed each of us with. None of us are perfect or without sin. When you are up to something good and Godly, the devil tries to keep you down. That special friend showed up in my time of despair to remind me of that fact. I knew that clearly, God sent him to deliver His message. No matter how many battles I face, God will always continue to send helpers. Our lives are ongoing journeys filled with lessons that bring us closer to God.

I know that the feeling of deep sadness from time to time is a natural part of who I am; they are the scars from a wound that may take a lifetime to heal. Learning how to be happy has always been difficult for me. However, I am pleased to say that I have come to realize that even when something in my life may seem bad it presents an opportunity for me to grow. It is through the walk in the valleys of life that allows us to rise.

As I see the light at the end of my valley, I am taking baby steps to learn how to be happy, in the moment, as it happens. A rebel by nature,

I have always had to hit rock bottom and become spiritually bankrupt before I became ready to embrace humility and gratitude.

Learning how to love myself has not been an easy task. God has shown me how to do things in stages. I had to reach the realization that I would have no inner peace until I learned to love myself unconditionally; the way that He does. It took all that I went through for me to understand that true beauty lies not on the outside, but deep within. My exterior body is just the shell that holds my authentic self.

Tied up in the molestation, the drug use and hitting rock bottom, I also began to gain weight, which was another catalyst that allowed me to wallow in self-hatred. I was happy when instead of obsessing on my weight issues, I began to tell myself how voluptuous and beautiful I am. I did that because I knew I needed to learn to love and accept myself regardless of what shape and size my body was in at that time. No matter how I look on the outside, I am still *me* on the inside. My exterior shell does not in any manner define who I am. The opportunity to improve is always there too, if I get uncomfortable with myself.

The most important lesson is focusing on my inner beauty and being the best person I can be. Inner peace has allowed me to own that reality and live a better life while maintaining the courage to continually pick myself up when needed. I now have that courage to love others unconditionally with no expectations because I love myself. Inner peace is the gold mine that I have always longed for. I am thrilled to realize it is now within my reach. I am even happier to know we all have the same treasure chest, one that contains every resource that we will ever need. That resource is God.

I also know now that healing is not a destination but a journey. There will never be an end to how we heal; it is an ongoing existence that we go through one day at a time. God will always continue to heal as long as we trust Him and practice faith.

I pray that this book reaches the hands of every little girl, boy, man and woman whose life may have been touched by any kind of abuse. In sharing my story, I hope you may never have to suffer as I have. If you believe that you have ever been violated, I urge you to find someone you can trust and talk to them so that you can begin your own healing journey.

In conclusion, I would like to say that whether you are a victim of abuse or not, we are all battling something in our lives. We all suffer, in some form or fashion, with something that wants to control us or define who we are. Being vulnerable is part of being human. God can show you the way to healing from self-destructive behaviors and feelings; all you need to do is open your heart in order to receive Him. At that point, you can believe that no matter how difficult your journey may be, there is a lesson and a blessing in it. Everything happens for a reason. In some cases, that reason is meant to be a tool to strengthen us into the vessel God intends us to be. We may never know what the blessing of the lesson is, unless we humble ourselves to the will of God. We must open up our ears long enough to truly listen as He speaks to us. Then and only then, will we truly see that God is ready to show us His love, as soon as we are ready to receive it.

I wish you all the blessings that God has to give, and I pray that you receive them now!

Parable of a Rose

"And God saw everything that He had made, and, behold, it was very good." — Genesis 1:31

When God completed the Heavens and the Earth, He had a very important meeting with the resident angels insisting that their attendance was mandatory. As the angels gathered around His golden throne, God instructed the head angel to give out their assignments, which were scribbled on fig leaves. He had just completed the finishing touches on creating the Earth, and it was time for the angels to get to work and fulfill their missions. As the angels accepted their leaves, one by one, from the head angel, God told them that He was sending each of them to earth with a very special assignment. They listened with anticipation as He informed them that the basis of determining whether they would be allowed to return and re-enter Heaven would be based solely upon how each angel completed their assignment. God reminded them that just like all of His other creations; angels were beautifully made for a unique purpose. As such, they would all be judged on three things; Love, Compassion and Forgiveness. He made it very clear that these were the things they were designed to instill in His children. Those three things would be the scale of contingency as a rule of measure for successful completion of their assignment.

After the meeting was adjourned, the angels began scrambling across the floor. Beautiful white feathers were flying in the air, and you could feel the excitement floating around them as they ran to go and prepare themselves for their pilgrimage to Earth.

85

God smiled.

He was happy.

The eagerness, in which they moved, brought Him joy.

As God surveyed the commotion, He noticed one angel whose wings were not spread eagle like the others. Her wings hung low and she was pacing and flipping her fig leaf back and forth. She looked as if she was confused about something so God called her over to His throne to find out what was troubling her.

The worried angel stared into the eyes of God and explained that she was not sure exactly what it was she needed to do, and that she desired His guidance in a manner that would give her the self-assurance she needed. She told God that she was afraid of her mission because she did not understand it.

She did not want to ruin any chances of being able to re-enter heaven due to failure on her part.

God looked into the worried eyes of His creation and all He could see therein was fear of failure. He knew he needed to reassure her.

Sometimes a Father has to mold a child into what they are destined to be. He summoned her to sit down beside Him, and He would explain exactly what He wanted her to do. She sighed with relief as she felt the warmth and comfort from His presence.

He explained that He had created her in His likeness, but He had also created her to represent a rose. A rose is the most beautiful of all flowers and appears to be fragile to the naked eye. However, the components within its makeup are where it's true beauty lies. The petals represent its delicate nature that is marked with a fine texture. When handled with the utmost respect and care it is pleasurable to all within its touch. The stem is where it draws its strength. That is the foundation of the rose and must always stay watered because that is the core of its existence. When nurtured properly, the stem stays strong and is the backbone of the rose. Do not be fooled by the thorns which appear on the stems, they are the protectors of the rose's beauty. The rose needs them to survive. They were placed there to prevent the flower from being mistreated and abused. One prick from them causes one to reconsider the way it will be touched again. Sometimes the rose forgets its own strength and does not tap into it, thus allowing the petals to wither and die.

This beautiful creation, a testament to both beauty and strength, comes in a vast array of colors of the rainbow and each color has a meaning. Red is the most prominent and significant, since it represents the meaning of love. As the rose completes its mission in life, the petals begin to descend freely. With each petal that falls from the stem, there will be a lesson learned about life. A rose never loses its own individual beauty, nor will it ever die because of its unique strength. The rose relaxes the mind, celebrates special occasions, and holds on to meaningful memories just by its very existence.

God smiled at the angel and let a few minutes of silence linger between them. He wanted her to absorb all that He had said before continuing.

Life on earth will come with many challenges, but remember to confront each one with love, compassion and forgiveness. That is your mission, do it in a manner that only you can. You are an angel; a messenger from Me to My people. You must speak the words that I cannot deliver to My children. Your mission is to be exactly what I have designed you to be. You are a beautiful rose; My gift to others. Remind My children, through the example of the rose that you are to be strong. Through love, compassion and forgiveness be a beacon of light and direction for My children who have lost their way. Give them love and remind them whose children they are. Let them also know that misery is only temporary and love is everlasting. Show them that compassion and understanding triumphs anything the world will tell them. Then run your fingers and embrace their entire being so that they will know forgiveness. If I am their Father and can forgive their shortcomings, then they should do the same for mortal man.

It won't be easy, My angel because life never is. Show them, through your actions that life is unfair; but it is necessary. Guide them to an understanding that some of the things that are endured, while ugly, have a purpose. Inject in them an understanding and confident assurance that trouble doesn't last always and there is a purpose in their pain.

You are My messenger. I need you to do your job in letting My children know that they are not alone, and that I see, hear, and know their pain. As you embark on your journey to fulfill your mission, always keep your spirit fed with prayer and the words I speak close to your heart.

I am God.

I will be the stem on the rose that you are; therefore, when you need to learn, do so, for you can always draw strength from Me.

God had given the angel all the information she needed to be well on her way. He kissed confidence on her forehead and leaned back on His throne knowing that He had reminded her to use the strength of a rose, and in doing so, He was assured that she would do just fine.

The angel turned back and looked into His eyes, and He knew that she understood her mission, her purpose and her design.

A tear rolled down her face as she raced off to catch up with the other angels. Three feathers fell from her wings, which were no longer hanging low, but were outstretched instead; they landed right near God's foot. He smiled to Himself knowing that the next time He would see her, her beautiful green eyes would no longer hold fear, uncertainty and self-doubt. He knew that when He saw her again she would have successfully completed the mission at hand and her eyes and aura would be filled with strength.

PART II

WE ARE NOT ALONE

OTHER VICTIMS SPEAK

Chapter Thirteen

Hannah's Story - Betrayal of a Father

It was my honor and privilege to interview a lovely and beautiful woman who is a survivor of sexual abuse. I've changed her name to Hannah in order to protect her identity; but the details of her story are true. I greatly appreciated the open and honest way in which she shared her story with me.

Hannah survived about five years of sexual abuse at the hands of her natural father. Since that time, she has worked hard to heal herself emotionally and to help other sexual abuse survivors heal as well. The mother of two boys, Hannah, who is married, spends much of her time running a women's ministry whose goal is to help women who are victims of abuse.

The oldest girl in a family of five brothers and four sisters, Hannah grew up in a home where the Pentecostal faith was strictly enforced and followed. Ironically, her father was the Preacher; the spiritual leader of their church. He was not only the head of her family; he was the shepherd of her religious teachings.

He began to abuse her sexually when she was fourteen or fifteen, as she recalls. If Hannah had trusted her father and wanted to please him before the abuse began, that all changed when she realized that what he was doing to her was wrong. Unsure about how to tell him to stop, she began to feel more and more ashamed until she reached the point where she hated herself; a feeling that destroyed her self-esteem.

Once she reached that point, Hannah began to believe his abuse was punishment for something she had done. She was confused because she was being abused by the one man who was supposed to protect her from the evils of the world. Hannah lived in a bubble of shame for being tainted goods. When she met her fiancé at the age of seventeen, she told him about the abuse and was very glad when he didn't walk away.

Hannah has shared her story here, in order to speak out to other survivors, letting them know that they are not alone, and to encourage them to begin to heal. Even though she endured great emotional pain and suffering, she believes it was her strong faith in God that allowed her to finally confront her father and move on with her life.

Hannah started out by saying that she'll never forget the way the abuse began:

"I started wearing makeup when I was in eighth grade. I'll never forget the first time my father touched me; putting his hands under my dress as I tried to put on my mascara. I remember how he'd touch me every time I tried to put it on, causing me to mess up, and I would have to wash it off and try to put it on, over and over again."

She went on to tell me how the abuse escalated from there:

I could see my father getting very nervous after my mother left for work each night, leaving me and my brothers and sisters alone with him. I'll never forget the night he waited until all my brothers, and sisters had gone to bed before calling me into the den, then telling me to lie down on the sofa.

I did so, of course, we always did what my father said. So, I laid down and listened as my father washed up in the bathroom for what seemed like a very long time. He came out, and then began to rub 'Noxzema' on my breasts. Then he rubbed it in, and around, for a very long time, rubbing my nipples as he did so. He moved down and then began to touch my vagina with his fingers.

When he was finally finished, he told me to go to bed.

I asked Hannah if she knew then that what he was doing was wrong.

I knew it was wrong. What I didn't know, at that point, was how to say, "Stop!" I always did whatever my father said. I had always wanted to please him. His sexual abuse confused me terribly, at that point. I was totally mixed up—I never knew what I was feeling, with one exception: I knew that the abuse was wrong—and he was wrong.

However, Hannah then confessed that she still had mixed feelings about the abuse. As an adolescent teen, her body was going through the normal changes of a girl of her age, and the physical sensations she experienced made her confused:

At one point in the abuse, I found myself in a place where I was looking forward to my father calling me into the room. Although I knew what he was doing was wrong, he'd awakened something in me, some part of my affections. He was my first-after all. So yes, at one point, I started waiting for him to call me, almost looking forward to it—which really confused me!

Fortunately, for Hannah, that feeling passed. After it did, the knowledge that what her father was doing to her was wrong. This motivated Hannah to tell her mother about the abuse:

I knew it was wrong—that was the main thing, but there were other reasons I told my mother as well. My father always liked to tell my mother how bad I'd been when she came home from work. What he didn't tell her is how he'd threaten me all the time, every night—then change his manner toward me completely as he began to abuse me yet again.

The sexual pleasure he took from my body seemed to make him happy, at least for a little while. That's why I believe I came to feel as though I was his mistress at some point. When I let him touch me, he treated me well.

In the midst of the continuous sexual abuse, Hannah told me that her father never used protection—making everything worse:

My father never used any sort of protection when he penetrated me; another cause for concern for me. If I close my eyes, I can still see the night he first put his penis in me—the first time in my life I ever saw a penis!

"Don't worry, you won't get pregnant." I remember him saying. Since I didn't know what else to do, I just blocked out everything I knew about how women got pregnant, so I could act as if I believed him.

The fact that Hannah's father was sexually active with her mother while he was sexually active with her complicated her situation—the victimization—even more:

My father was sleeping with my mother at the same time he was sleeping with me, a situation that caused me to feel even more upset and confused. The abuse had gone on for a number of years at that point; meanwhile, I had met the man who became my fiancé. I felt emotionally committed to him and torn while my father was having sex with me.

It was no wonder that I developed some big emotional problems when I found out my mother was pregnant. It could have been me—that was my first thought. Becoming pregnant by my father was my greatest fear; something I knew I could never accept. If I had my father's child, how could I ever tell that child who his or her father was? That question troubled me terribly.

That was also why I thanked God it wasn't me who had gotten pregnant. I developed some very strange feelings about my mother at that time, as well as for my father. The strongest feeling concerning my mother was that of jealousy. If I was my father's mistress, who I often felt I was, and she was his wife, my jealousy was understandable. Although my mother and I had never been too close, major problems soon developed in our relationship.

I asked Hannah if she thought her mother knew her father was having sex with her:

I don't believe she did, but I also believed she should have known or have seen some signs. That was why I couldn't understand my mother or bond with her, a situation that continued well into adulthood. At the same time, I also believed my mother hated me but would never admit it. At least one of my siblings, my sister, noticed that too.

"You and mommy don't act like mother and daughter; you act like strangers," she once told me. It was at that point that I realized my suspicions that my mother hated me might well be based on fact. I couldn't help but notice how disgusted she always seemed whenever we were together, and it confirmed the suspicion in my mind.

Looking back, I wish I could have talked to her at that time. I just didn't know how to do that.

Hannah and I then discussed the way she felt about her family's church, during the time she was being abused:

The abuse caused me lots of problems when I went to church. Some of those problems stayed with me well into adulthood. Specifically, people give hugs in church and for the longest time, I'd just shrink away, especially if a man tried to hug me. As a married woman, I often asked my husband, "Please tell the men to stop hugging the women!"

I realized I was being unfair, putting MY issues on everyone else. I also realized that the fact that I couldn't hug others was just another part of my own self- hatred. "God help me!" I said, one day, "How did I get this way?"

I had a particularly bad time in the church one day when I went to shake hands with a brother, and he said, "Oh no, we don't do that here— we hug." All I could think of at that point, was, Oh my God, help me, Lord help me!

An even worse incident occurred when a preacher friend of my father's grabbed me from behind and held me so tight. I could feel his manhood in my back. I felt myself just flip out, at that point.

Hugging can still bring it all back, sometimes.

Hannah went on to talk about the reasons she and her husband left her father's church years after the abuse:

I was in therapy, and my husband was going with me, when the therapist asked, "Why do you and Hannah still go to her father's church? I can understand why Hannah would go when she was younger, but now that you're grown—married with children—why do you keep going there?"

We gave that question lots of thought before we decided to make a change. We don't go to my father's church, not anymore. There was also a long period of time when I wouldn't go to my mom's house because a lot of the abuse happened in the basement. Sometimes, I could almost see her thinking, "What's your problem?" But every time I went there, the smell of the house, especially the basement, would just drive me away.

In an attempt to get a clearer understanding of the dynamics of Hannah's home life, I went on to ask her about her relationships with her siblings at the time of the abuse:

I wasn't the only one of my siblings my father abused. I know for sure he also abused one of my sisters. I suspect he may have abused some of the others, too. I just don't know for sure because no one ever talked about it, not even the sister who was being abused.

I did tell some of my siblings about the abuse, but I didn't do that until it had ended. Two of my brothers and one of my sisters believed me when I told them, which didn't matter to me as much as the fact that it felt like my family was going haywire, with all those secrets going on. What made it even worse was the fact that publicly, we all seemed to be able to keep up the image of a normal, happy and healthy family. However, in private, that image was far from the truth—we were all keeping too many secrets, and all of those secrets were dark.

When I confronted my family, those secrets came out—quickly, almost like the beginning of a snowball effect.

The fact was I had walked around in shame for too long. When it comes to abuse, if the shame doesn't kill you, the guilt will. I walked with my head held down. For years, I would never look at anybody because I thought that when people looked at me, they'd know I'd been abused.

I knew for sure I always looked sad, all the time, so many people commented on it. I think they knew something was wrong, but they didn't know what. I felt like nobody wanted me, and I wasn't good enough for anybody. In fact, I believe that's why I try so hard to succeed today.

Hannah and I began to discuss the problems with her mother; problems that had a profound effect on her life. Some of those problems are still with her:

In light of my problems with my mother, I soon began to feel like I didn't fit in when it came to my family. As many brothers and sisters as we had, all growing up in such close proximity to each other, I never got over the feeling that I was always on the outside looking in. I also constantly felt a strong, undeniable need to be by myself, even if I just went into a different room, or another part of the same room. Even today, I seldom have a feeling of missing my brothers and sisters because of the way I always needed my own space.

I still need my space to this day; I don't like to feel crowded in, not anywhere, by anyone.

As a young adult, Hannah finally worked up the courage to tell her mother about the abuse from her father. I asked how her mother reacted:

Looking back, I feel now that I shouldn't have been as blunt with the truth as I was--I should have found a gentler way to tell her. Maybe that would've helped, maybe not. My mom and I are still in the early stages of healing, and my mom has told me she thinks she's okay with it now, but I don't really believe it. She prays a lot; she still feels deeply committed to her church, my father's church.

I tell my mother often that in situations like this you need to do more than pray. However, she just shakes her head. "Let's pray about it some more." That's what she always says, and she believes it will heal her, heal us. I do not share that same sentiment.

Prayer does help—I know that. I also know that everyone needs to do their own work on their problems. For myself, I don't want to take my problems to my grave. I believe that exposing the problems, bringing them out into the open and dealing with them is the only way to stop the devil and destroy his power.

I asked Hannah how the abuse impacted her relationship with the man who became her husband:

The confusion caused by the abuse got worse, as time went on. At the age of 17, my family and I were still going to church; my father was still the spiritual leader there, too. I worked at the church and also sang in the choir. The ironies of this situation got to be too much for me to bear by myself, at some point. That was when I told my fiancé about the abuse.

He didn't say anything at all; not at first. He just sort of looked shocked, took a step back and kind of fell against the wall. If I'd expected him to walk away, I was happier than words can say that he didn't. That's why, looking back, I know it was then that I began to see him as my Knight in Shining Armor, the man who could help rescue me.

The abuse still continued. My father and I didn't have intercourse every night, but he was still abusing me a few times a week. And he still didn't use a condom, the reason that my fear of getting pregnant soon began to consume me. I had also begun to feel a strong, though inappropriate attachment to him; I was really having a hard time separating from him— crazy!

My feelings about myself, meanwhile, continued to spiral downward. I didn't think I was good enough and always asked myself, "What did I do?" Because I thought I had to do something to make my father do this to me. I was hard on myself and beat myself up all the time. I didn't think I was good enough for anything, or anyone; another reason I was glad when my fiancé stuck by me.

I felt so terribly wrong, all the time, so terribly damaged. Nothing mattered to me, at that point, because I didn't matter. I couldn't understand how anyone else could love me when there was something so very wrong with me.

I asked Hannah what happened then:

My self-hatred built and built; it climaxed when I was 22, a young married woman. It was then that I decided I wanted to take my own life by committing suicide. My husband and I were not doing well with our relationship at that time. One day, I grabbed the keys to our car and drove out to Routes 1 and 9, a heavily-traveled road. I pulled out and put my foot all the way down on the gas and then drove that car as fast as it would go, hoping to hit a brick wall. I wanted to end the pain, a pain so intense, no words could ever describe it.

Then, suddenly, something told me, "Don't do it!" I don't know why I listened to that voice, but I did.

Hannah went on to tell me more about the role her husband played, in helping her begin to heal:

I married young, and I definitely got married to get out of my house and away from my father, a situation my husband was aware of, as I said. Nevertheless, he always stuck by me, the reason I can say he was the wind beneath my wings, the man who helped save my life. The fact that

I'd never had anyone in my life that was ever willing to do that made it even better. I will always be grateful for that—and for my husband's love and support.

It wasn't easy for him either. Mood swings are one of the after effects of surviving sexual abuse. I was happy one minute and sad the next—difficult for my husband to deal with. I confronted my father on that fact, too, later on, telling him how he almost ruined my marriage.

Another effect of the abuse was the fact that for years, I would never let my husband see me naked. When I went to take a shower, I'd take all my clothes into the bathroom and came out fully dressed. This went on for a long time.

Hannah went on to discuss other ways in which the abuse affected her family life, specifically her relationship with her son:

I found it hard to warm up to my son. I was uncomfortable holding him; for example, because deep down, I was afraid I might do the same thing to him that my father had done to me. It was a deep down feeling, as I said, that was always in the back of my mind. I just couldn't feel sure that I wouldn't do it—a feeling that made me afraid to get close to him. I never, ever wanted to hurt him the same way my father had hurt me.

I really didn't know how to bond with him—or anyone else, either; another result of the abuse, another thing I had to deal with. In fact, both my sons were teenagers before I started hugging them.

Hannah went on to discuss the point at which she began to seek professional help for her problems:

I was married, in my mid-30's, driving down to Virginia with one of my sons. I was in my car when I realized that I was sick and tired of the pain that was always with me and draining me. I felt sick all the time; sick and angry enough to curse a lot. I was sad most of the time, too and all I did was cry.

I didn't trust other people either. I didn't trust anyone. I'd developed a pattern of sabotaging relationships before people could get close to me--before they could hurt me--something I was sure everyone wanted to do. That was why, I told myself I had to get them before they got to me.

By the time I reached my cousin's house in Virginia, I told her I was through with the pain—I wanted and needed to put it behind me. I threw myself into her arms and began to sob.

"You need professional help, Hannah," she told me gently. Hours later, after I settled down, prayed on it and reached the conclusion that if it was meant for me to get professional help, the right person would be put in my path to help me.

After I got home, I found "The Shepherd's Guide," a book that had names and numbers of spiritual advisors in it. I picked one number and called it, then left a message with my name and phone number. Someone called me back about 20 minutes later. That was when I began to get help.

Hannah went on to discuss the point in her recovery when she confronted her father:

I always wanted to confront my father, but I didn't think I was ready to do that when I began therapy. My therapist confirmed that feeling. I'd been working with my therapist for several years before he told me the time had come. I was ready to confront my father, he said; then he added that I had to do it alone. He didn't want me to have anybody with me when I did it, because it was MY power, I was taking back from the man who had abused me.

I made an appointment to meet with my dad, and I didn't take anybody with me, not even my husband. "I have to talk to you," I told my father when he met me at his church.

It was at that point, that I remembered the therapist had told me to make sure he looked me in the eye. At that moment, my father couldn't look at me at all.

I debated whether to go on with what I had to say or not, but I knew I wanted to tell him we were leaving his church. I also felt sure that I'd never go back to confront him after we'd left, so I had to do it right then and there, if I wanted to close that chapter of my life once and for all.

My father still wouldn't look at me when I asked him to. Then something came over me, and I screamed: "Look at me!" It worked, he finally looked me in the eye. A look that made me shiver, because all I could see in his eyes was the devil.

I forced myself to go on. I told him how he'd made me feel and asked all the questions that had rolled around inside me for so many years— why did you do it, why did you hate me so much? I asked all the questions that were on my mind. We talked for a long time; then I went home and cried like a baby.

I felt better after I left—I knew I'd taken my power back. My father seemed angry that I'd confronted him. At least he did answer some of my questions by saying, "It wasn't your fault. It wasn't anything you did."

I wished he had said he was sorry, but he never did. I was not happy with that, but I told myself that maybe God didn't think it was time yet. Years later, I found out, I was right. When I went to see my father on his deathbed, I told him, "You need to apologize to me before you go home," and he did so.

Everything in its own time...

We talked about her feelings about her father then:

The strangest thing was I never hated my father. His abuse caused me a great deal of pain, but I never hated him. My therapist kept saying, "You have to hate your father."

"I can't." That was always my reply.

"You have to," he'd say. I would never let myself hate him. I felt confused, and I also felt pity for him, but I never hated him.

Hannah and I went on to discuss our similar spiritual journeys; the journeys that helped us both heal. I told her how grateful I was that God brought us this far in our journeys, because our stories could definitely have ended very differently. She replied:

Yes, we could have gone to our graves without anyone knowing what happened to us and how much it affected us and the lives we live. One thing I want to say that really helped me was my faith in God and my relationship with Him. I remember the therapist told me, "Hannah, the only reason you didn't lose your mind is because you love the Lord."

One thing the abuse did was teach me how to put my trust in the Lord. One scripture that I always remember, and think of often: "I am a healer of all my people."

I asked Hannah if she had ever doubted God, or her relationship with Him.

I hated God when the abuse was happening to me. I remember crying like a crazy woman and telling God how much I hated Him at one point when I was married.

"How can you call yourself a God and let this happen to me?" That was the question I asked Him because I absolutely did not feel loved by God. Those doubts can really mess with you. I worked it through. Looking back, I know now how much He helped me.

I asked Hannah how she found her faith again:

When my husband started counseling, and we moved to another city, he'd always ask me why I was crying. I never knew how to answer him; I didn't even know why I was crying most of the time, that's how bad it got.

"Start prayer--,"that's what I was told when I asked the Spirit for help. I would have prayer by myself. I would go to prayer on Monday and Tuesday with some other prayer partners, and on Wednesdays I would have my own prayer again, about 10 o'clock. There were also days when I went to church and found that I couldn't pray—I could only cry.

It felt so bad, that one day I went up on the altar, curled myself into a fetal position and just cried and cried. I did that for years, but I never stopped going to church--never stopped trying to heal.

Looking back, I can say that praying, reading lots of self-help books and going to counseling is what helped me to get my deliverance. Psalms 139:14 is one of the scriptures that really helped me: "I will praise You, for I am fearfully and wonderfully made." Marvelous are Your works, and that my soul knows very well. Psalms 103:3 was also special to me: "Who forgiveth all thine iniquities; who healeth all thy diseases."

I'm more thankful than words can say, that I can testify to the fact that yes, He is a healer.

At this point, I asked Hannah how her own strong spirituality helped her to help other sexual abuse survivors:

I thank God that when I see other sisters I can pick up whether or not they're abuse survivors. There was one little girl, about 14, and she just fell against my chest and cried. All I could do was hold her and tell her, "It's gonna' be all right."

I knew I really had to do something; we all really have to do something, because there are so many abuse victims.

I shared a little about my own feelings with Hannah then, as being one of those survivors:

So many survivors—more than we know. It happens so much! In so many cultures, what happens in the family stays in the family. Then these patterns of abuse just continue to repeat themselves, and it never gets reported. People don't go for help either. I mean, back in the day, people never thought about therapy. Therapy wasn't popular even during the time when I grew up. If you went to therapy, you were crazy—there was always a strong, definite stigma, when it came to getting counseling.

Hannah went on then:

Counseling was a stigma, even in the church. If you went to therapy, people would tell you "Get on your knees and PRAY!" Prayer is important, but it's not enough. Talking about it—that's just as important. That's why we have small groups in our women's ministry. We're trying to get the women to open up and talk, but too often, they won't. When that happens, we just continue to work with them and to try to chip away at all their issues.

I began speaking with Hannah more about my own trust issues, at that point:

I know I've fought with trust issues, issues I had with people I looked up to, people I've trusted with all my heart—people who violated that trust.

"If I can't trust those people, who CAN I trust?" That was the question I asked myself over and over again. Violation distorted my perception of trust. So, of course it took a long, long time to rebuild that trust before I could talk to anyone about what happened to me; before I could even begin to tell anyone all the secrets that I had kept inside for far too long.

I went on to ask Hannah if she'd succeeded at feeling good about herself, and if so, how she managed to get pass her feelings of self-hatred:

103

"Oh yeah, I feel good about myself! I went to counseling for six years—that was important, almost as important as God's help in healing me.

There were times when I minimized the abuse when I went to counseling. "It really wasn't that bad." That's what I told myself. Although, deep down, I knew it was bad—very bad. Even today, there are still some things I don't remember. I guess that's a good thing.

I shared my own views about healing with Hannah:

I believe therapy is very beneficial, not only for the survivor, but also for anyone else who is associated with the victim or has been affected by the abuse. I know how common it is for people to sweep the abuse under the rug, hoping it will go away, because no one wants to deal with it. It's hard to heal from something that you've hidden for so many years.

That's why faith is so important and such a big part–a spiritual part–of this book too, because that's what really helped me heal. I couldn't have even begun to heal until I could trust again and believe that God could make a difference and change all things.

I thanked Hannah for taking the time to speak with me, and we both agreed that it had been a good interview and a cathartic experience for us both.

Chapter Fourteen

Dominique's Story
Sexual Abuse From A Different Perspective

I had mixed feelings when I received word from the New Jersey Department of Corrections that I'd been approved to interview a convicted sex offender. I felt happy that I was making progress towards my goal of raising awareness about sexual abuse; but the idea of interviewing a convicted sex offender just felt surreal, somehow.

Was I really going to do it?

Would I really be all right?

I could not let fear stop me from accomplishing the mission I was supposed to fulfill. That meant stepping into territory I was uncomfortable crossing into. It was necessary to hear about sexual abuse from the other side—from someone who had been a perpetrator in causing abuse—but I had some feelings of fear because I did not know what to expect in doing so. In the end, I trusted God to guide me. Since I wasn't at all sure what to expect, I still felt a little apprehensive.

I also realized that this interview might well provide an opportunity for a breakthrough in my own personal healing process, since it would help me to determine if this was the work I really wanted to pursue.

My project—this book—had taken on a life of its own, with more unexpected twists and turns than I could count. However, those surprises did not upset me, since I felt certain that God was leading me where He needed me to go—on a journey that would help me touch the people who needed it most, and help heal their souls.

It has been a wonderful journey, but it was never easy. Some days, realizing that I was exposing my life and feelings to the world filled me with enough anxiety to trigger a few full-fledged panic attacks. Other nights, I sat up wondering if people would judge me when they learned what had happened to me. Even though I knew that telling my story was the right thing to do, I still felt as if someone or something was opposing me.

You've come this far, I would tell myself when those thoughts arose. No turning back!

I knew, at that point, that this book was not only about the injustices that had happened to me. It was much bigger than that. A sense of calm came over me, reassuring me that I was doing the right thing. My candidness was necessary and important in order for the message to be heard. I wanted—and needed— to be a voice that could be heard for millions of other voices that had been silenced by guilt and shame. That was when it became crystal clear—God wanted me to do this, and He would support me through it all, never giving me more than I could handle.

The interview below took place at the Adult Diagnostic Treatment Center (ADTC) in Avenel, New Jersey; a prison that houses and provides treatment for approximately 767 male sex offenders. Dominique is a 33-year old Hispanic/African-American male who volunteered to tell his story. His name has been changed to protect his identity.

When I first met Dominique, I found him to be articulate and polite— just a regular guy. He had received a 20-year sentence for sexually abusing his sister and his son. He had already served ten years of that sentence when I met him; eight of which were spent at ADTC.

He said he wanted to be included in my project in order to put out some positive energy to help people who suffer from the effects of having been sexually abused.

Dominique is one of three children, with one older brother and a younger sister who was almost a decade younger than him. He always believed his father showed favoritism towards his sister, which made him resentful and angry.

Dominique began talking to me with an explanation of why he had agreed to be interviewed:

My life has taught me a lot. When I think about all the energy I spent on the street, doing things I shouldn't have been doing, I decided to try to turn it around by putting out some positive energy that might help me and others.

I thanked him again for agreeing to do the interview and went on to explain that I believed a sex offender's view of sexual abuse would help give my book some balance. I asked him, if there had been any sexual trauma in his life, a common factor, which motivates many sexual offenders. He told me yes; he had experienced sexual trauma as a young boy. He began his story by telling me more about his childhood and the first time his cousin sexually abused him:

I was born in Italy. My family was in the military, so we moved around a lot. We lived abroad until we moved to New Jersey in 1979, where we lived on base. Then we moved back to Europe in 1986 and stayed there another three years. We moved back to New Jersey in 1990, and I've been here ever since.

My father retired from the military and is now a church pastor. My mother is a school teacher. I am their middle child, with an older brother and a younger sister.

Looking back, I would say I grew up in an ideal, almost perfect family. We ate our meals together, took family vacations and even had family meetings every Friday. I had a happy childhood until the day I found out my father had cheated on my mother, something that sent a huge negative ripple through all of our lives.

It was then that we went down to visit my aunt, uncle and cousins in Baltimore one weekend; something we had done before. Whenever we went down there, we'd always take showers on Saturday night to get ready for church on Sunday morning.

That weekend, when my cousin, who was nine at the time, suggested we shower together, I agreed to do so. He suggested we practice some of the wrestling moves we had seen on TV in the shower. It was at that point that he started touching me between my legs, and then put me on top of him, where he began to tickle and fondle me.

I wasn't sure what was going on. Many different feelings ran through my head when my aunt called us to get out of the shower. We went to his room to get dressed, but my cousin wanted to keep on wrestling. I agreed, but I never expected to end up on his bed, where he made me give him oral sex.

Sex in general was very secretive back then. However, as exciting as it was, this kind of sex did not feel good to me. When I told him I wanted to stop, he agreed. Then we both went to sleep.

The next day after church, in my grandfather's house, my cousin tried to rape me. I was in the bedroom taking off my Sunday clothes when he came from behind and bent me over the bed, then pulled my underwear down and got ready to penetrate me. Fortunately, my grandfather came up, and asked what we were doing. I was trembling, but my cousin was cool and collected. "Just playing around," he told my grandfather, who believed him and went out of the room.

Later, as we were going downstairs, my cousin leaned over and whispered in my ear, "Gotcha'!" It was at that point that I got scared. I tried to stay around the rest of the family for the remainder of the weekend because I didn't want to be alone with my cousin.

He somehow managed to get me alone later that day. We were downstairs playing Twister when he asked me to put my hands on him. I didn't want to do it, but I didn't want to challenge him either. He was older than I was and bigger too. I couldn't help but feel a bit afraid of him. I ended up giving him more oral sex that day. I'd put my clothes back on by the time my brother came downstairs, so he never realized what had gone on.

Dominique went on to say how his mother spoke to him about sex three years later, right before the family was scheduled to move back to Europe:

I was almost 10 years old when my mother said, "Let's go down to the library and get some books on sex education."

After we went to the library, she asked if I had any questions. That was when I remembered what my cousin had done to me. "What if someone puts their hands on you, and you don't like it?" I asked her.

My mother just shook her head. "Dominique," she said, "There's always something going on with you—it's always about you. What about me—and the fact that your father cheated on me?" She asked—before she burst into tears.

Bad news! If I had any hope of telling her how my cousin had abused me; it went right out the door, and I knew then it wasn't going to happen. Meanwhile, she was still crying. I did my best to console her. I gave her a hug. Privately, I also made up in my mind that there was no sense telling anyone what had happened to me or how it made me feel.

I asked Dominique if the abuse had continued in those three years between the time it first happened and when the family's moved back to Europe. He replied:

No, it was only those two times that weekend. Thankfully, after that, we stopped going to Baltimore.

Dominique, as if in a trance, went on to tell me more about his family's move to Europe:

We moved to Europe then—away from all my friends. However, my brother and I still felt the move was a good thing. There was so much chaos in our family then. We felt the move would give all of us a new beginning. My brother and I really hoped things would get better.

Our first six months abroad were wonderful. My father would take us to breakfast every Saturday morning, and me and my mother actually began to get along pretty well. Everything was going fine until my father received some notoriety from him being a minister while serving in the military. At that point, we were back to square one. The family no longer ate together as much; there was less communication. It was around that time that my sister was born; adding a whole new set of problems to our lives.

Dominique described one example of those problems:

I remember one time when I had football practice. We lived in a German neighborhood, about 20 minutes away from the American neighborhood. It took a good 30 minutes to get to football practice.

One night after practice, the coach offered to drive me home when no one came to pick me up. I assured him my mother would be there, but practice ended at seven o'clock and she didn't show up until eight thirty. It was raining that night and I was crying by the time she got there.

"I'm sorry, Dominique, I forgot about you," she said. Those words hurt me deeply. I felt like nobody cared. I went to my room, as soon as we got home. I felt like no one could hurt me there; it was my own personal, protective cocoon.

It was at that point that I began to question if my new baby sister was, in fact, really my sister. My father had spoken to me before she was born, telling me, "Listen, this is your sister. So whatever you're thinking, you can't do it."

I still don't know exactly what he was thinking, or how he even came up with feeling the need to say what he said, but I do remember the way he was always protecting her.

"Oh, that's a princess, there! Nobody's going to lay a hand on my Princess," he'd say over and over again, when she was born. Each time he said it, it made me feel angry, resentful and disconnected. Very simply, I felt as if I had lost my father, the parent I was closest to, since I had never gotten along that well with my mother.

Nor did my mother and father get along at that time. If my father told me to come home at 8:00, for example, my mother might say, "Come home at 8:30." They were always giving me those kinds of mixed messages.

That was why after my sister was born, and was clearly favored by my father, I started to believe I might not be my parents' natural child; instead, I believed I was adopted. That was why whenever my parents went out, I'd go through their drawers trying to find proof of my adoption. Because if I really had been adopted, at least that would explain what was going on and why I felt so disconnected, as if I was the black sheep of the family.

Dominique went on to explain how his racial heritage, and skin color, reinforced those feelings within him:

My family was mixed. My mother was African-American and my father was a dark-skinned Hispanic. In terms of color, my mother was lighter than me and my brother was also light-skinned, with green eyes. I was definitely the darkest-skinned person in the family, which was the main reason I believed I really might have been adopted.

Dominique never found any evidence to show that was the case, but after his sister was born and favored by his father; his growing resentment resulted in more problems:

I was nine when my sister was born. I soon began to resent my father. With my new baby sister getting all his attention, I felt unloved, ignored and neglected. I began to ask myself how I could regain my father's attention and love. That was when I started looking at my sister in a sexual way.

The house was set up so that you had to go through my sister's room to get to my parents' room and my room too. Meanwhile, I had begun to drink alcohol. That happened when my parents' landlord asked me to take care of the horses he kept in back of the house. He would reward me by letting me ride them and also giving me a key to his liquor cabinet. The rules about sex, drugs and alcohol were a lot more lenient in Europe than they were in the United States. So drinking at that age was not frowned upon.

In any case, whenever my parents kept me up at night with their arguments, I would escape to my landlord's place—and his liquor. Although, being by myself at those times were just as important to me as drinking the liquor.

This went on for a couple of years. I was 11 when I noticed his VCR player and a shelf with some videotapes on it. I put one of the tapes in that night. It was a porno tape. I was soon watching the tapes often, and no one knew I was doing it. I never expected how quickly the tapes would trigger sexual feelings in me, and yet at the same time they triggered shame for having those feelings.

Those feelings eventually caused Dominique to begin to abuse his little sister, and he explained how that came about:

One night after I had a few drinks and watched a porno video at my landlord's house, I went through my sister's room to get to my own room. I saw her lying in bed; she was three years old at that time.

It was a hot night, and I remember looking at her, sexually, for the first time. Those sexual thoughts did not make me happy, and I tried to repress them. I told myself to keep right on going past her room. However, that night, when I got to my room, I masturbated to the fantasy of molesting my sister.

The next morning, my mother had a huge argument with my father and slapped him so hard it left marks on his face, and he left. That made me so angry, something deep inside me snapped.

I went into my sister's room and asked her if she wanted to come into my room to play a video game. She said okay and was wearing a long t-shirt that day. I used the same tactics with her that my cousin had used with me. Looking back, it embarrasses me to say it, but I laid her down on her stomach and said "C'mon, let's wrestle."

Then I took her shirt off and pulled her panties down. I took out my penis and moved back and forth between the cheeks of her backside until I came. I got up afterwards and pretended everything was okay.

She left without another word and the rest of that day went on as if nothing unusual had happened. I never planned to do it again. However, a few weeks later, that's exactly what happened. This time, it was late afternoon and my father came home unexpectedly and caught me molesting my sister.

"What are you doing? What's going on?" he demanded. The answer was simple; he and I both knew what I was doing. I remember screaming out: "This is wrong— I need help!"

I never expected my father's reply: "No, it's just your hormones. You're 11 years old, in a new country—experiencing different things." I guessed that meant he was okay with what I had done, which was important to me because my father's word was the law back then. Nor was there any punishment or repercussion for what I had done. I was still nervous about what might happen if I ever did it again, that was the reason why I never did. Well, at least not while we were living in Europe.

Dominique's family returned to New Jersey three years later, when he was 14 and his sister was 5 or 6. He talked about the family's return and the return of his abuse of his sister:

One night after our move back my parents had to go to a military ball. My father asked me to watch my sister. I agreed although in the back of my mind, I knew I should not be alone with her. Since it was my father who had asked, I thought it must be okay.

However, that turned out not to be the case. The same thing happened that night that had happened in Europe. I brought her up to my bedroom and molested her.

I asked her if she was frightened.

She wasn't scared because I made it feel like a game, the "under the covers game," that's what I called it. So as soon as I suggested we play, she agreed. I hate to say it, but I guess I had trained her, bringing her to the point where it all seemed normal. Meanwhile, deep inside, I told myself that even though my father might think of her as his Princess, really, she was as low as I was because she never put up a fight or resisted me in any way.

I wrestled with that issue, but not for long. Everything felt alright until my parents came home. My sister was in the bathroom when they noticed her underwear was inside out.

"Did you do it again?" my father asked. When I said yes, he replied that he thought he should send me to a detention center for boys.

"Hold on, three years ago it wasn't an issue but now suddenly it is?" I replied. Looking back, I know how manipulative that was. I knew I was essentially blackmailing my father in terms of affecting his strong, very positive public image.

At that time, my father was really tight with the general who lived on the Army base. So when he threatened to send me away, I knew he would have to ask the General for permission, something he would never, ever, do because that would reveal our family's problems.

That was why he walked out of my room, slamming the door behind him. After that, we didn't speak to each other for the next week.

I asked Dominique where his brother was at the time all of this was going on, and how he was involved in the situation.

My brother knew what was going on; everyone did. They swept it under the rug; it was a huge family secret. Nobody talked about it because the last thing my parents wanted was for that kind of truth to ever get out. That was the way my father was raised—never air dirty family laundry.

Another strange thing was that my parents were very strict with us as we were growing up. All of our lives, everyone whom we had known and everything we did, had to be connected with the church. That was a very strong foundation for my family.

My father was also such a regimented person, probably from being in the military, he insisted we keep to a firm schedule even in the summer. I remember several years when we had vacation Bible school from 9 to 11, homework from 12 to 4, and more Bible school from 6 to 8 at night.

My father directed our church attendance on Sundays just as rigidly. We couldn't sit in the pews with our friends; we had to sit with the family. If there was anything scheduled after church, we had to go to that too.

At some point, I felt lonely; then I got angry over it. I felt very isolated at this point. My father always told us we couldn't trust anyone outside the family. Since I wasn't getting along with anyone in my family, at that time, I just began to spend a lot of time in my room, the room I had started to think of as my sanctuary.

Dominique went on to explain how that feeling of isolation had begun after his cousin molested him, which was also right around the same time his father cheated on his mother:

Everything went downhill after my cousin raped me. We were a happy family before that happened. My parents would always say how lucky they were to have children like us. However, things changed when my father cheated on my mother with the choir director. Both caused all kinds of problems among us, and I felt like we were five strangers living in the same house.

WITHOUT PERMISSION

It got so bad that sometimes, my mother would pack us up in the car and drive around New Jersey looking for a new church to attend. We were Baptist, so those were the churches we went to. No matter where we went, we soon found that they knew who my father was and respected him.

Dominique went back to talking about the way he molested his sister. I asked how he felt about what he had done as he looked back on it. Then we went on to the subject of forgiveness:

Looking back on that part of my life, I am extremely embarrassed. I also feel lots of guilt and remorse because I took out my painful feelings on an innocent person; someone who did not deserve it, someone who didn't even know what was going on.

I felt blessed, four or five years ago, when they had a Family Day here and my mother and my sister, who was 18 at that time, came up. When my mother went to use the bathroom, my sister told me she forgave me.

"You shouldn't be saying that," I wanted to tell her. "You should be cursing me out."

It really wasn't about her. The problem was I had never forgiven myself for what I had done. I'm very thankful today that my sister and I have a solid relationship. I still have lots of regret and guilt; I know I never should have done it.

At that point, I asked Dominique if he felt he would ever be able to forgive himself for what he had done.

I'm in that stage now, and I'm trying my best. I'm not all the way there, not yet.

I went on to ask him if he felt he could ever forgive his cousin.

That's still a sore spot, but I know that if I were to see him again, I could never refuse to speak to him. It would also be tough to stay mad at him when my own sister has forgiven me. That would be selfish on my part.

"If she can forgive me, why can't I forgive him?" I ask myself that question often—that's how I'm working on forgiving him. I want to let it go, whether I ever see him again or not. I want to be in that place of forgiveness.

115

Dominique went on to tell me more about his relationships with others, including the mother of his children:

I was 16 when I met this girl, and we began to have a relationship outside the church. She and I were very involved with each other for the next six years. When I was 17 and she was 19, we had our first child out of wedlock. Of course, my father didn't like that. I didn't like the way he acted when he first found out she was pregnant. After spending so much of his life preaching against abortion, I was stunned when he told me privately, one day, that he thought this woman should go out and do just that—abort our child.

Our son was the first born of our two children. Unfortunately, our relationship was never easy. We both ran away right before having our first baby because neither of our families could accept our relationship. Our family was upscale and prestigious. Everyone knew and respected my father.

My girlfriend came from a very different kind of family, with a mother who was always in and out of jail. Part of the reason I loved her had to do with the fact that she was definitely someone I could rescue. I loved the way she looked up to me and my family because of who we were and how much we had. Very few people had ever looked up to me before— for any reason.

After we ran away and before our son was born, we lived with a friend. It was at that time that my father got me a job working in a warehouse, making pretty good money, enough to enable us to move out and finally get our own place.

I remember the night I brought my son over to my family's house. My mother looked at us and said, "I'm going to treat my grandson the way I should have treated you." I thought that was great. It also made me feel that yes, it may be possible to have a relationship with my mother. Maybe it wasn't too late for us to bond.

Unfortunately, it never happened, maybe because of all the other stuff that was going on. Including the way I had dropped out of high school, so I could get a job that would provide for my new family. In any case, we lived five minutes away from my family, but there was no communication. They never came over to the apartment where I lived or anything like that.

That hurt me. Not to mention, I felt really devastated when my parents got an *ADT* security system and gave the code to my brother, but not to me.

That action on their part brought all the old feelings back. I was 20 by then, with a good job that had suddenly begun to feel like a dead end. That was why I went to see an Air Force recruiter, who agreed to help me study for my GED, so I could enlist. I was doing that when my girlfriend and I began to have problems.

We were living together with a new baby, and I wanted sex all the time. As the breadwinner, I felt entitled to it—that was what we argued about most of the time. "If you love me, you'll have sex with me," I'd tell her.

"Why can't we just talk?" She would ask. She wanted more from the relationship than only sex, something that was really hard for me to understand.

I asked Dominique how the arguments made him feel and also how they ended.

We reached one point where I told her if she didn't give me sex, I'd go out and get it somewhere else. She started crying then and gave me sex that night. However, the fact that I had to threaten her with infidelity in order to get it didn't sit well with me. I had always considered myself ugly because I had a good-looking, light-skinned, green-eyed brother who seemed to get all the attention.

Maybe that's why I felt I had to prove a point when my girlfriend didn't give me sex. Lots of older women were looking at me, at that point, and it felt so good. I ran with it and stayed out with other women every night, before going home. When my girlfriend asked me where I had been, I lied and told her I was out with the guys. In fact, I was cheating on her. I justified it by telling myself I was still young, with lots of women paying attention to me. Most of the time, my girlfriend and I argued and fought. Our problems got worse as I cheated more and more, until I became really arrogant. I still felt like I was competing with my brother because I was having sex with some women his age. I also felt like I was competing with my father, who had done the same thing to my mom.

Dominique continued recollecting about that time in his life as he told me how his father called him out on his behavior:

My father called me in one day to tell me how upset my girlfriend was with me, since I was hardly ever home. He wanted to know what was going on with me. The fact that he cheated on my mother, made me very angry with him. "How can you tell me I need to be there for my own family when I can't even get into your house? There have been issues between us—big ones—ever since I was a kid."

He tried to bring the focus back to me and my current relationship; but I wasn't having any of that. I walked out and slammed the door behind me.

Then I went home and gave my girlfriend a sob story; "I apologize for the things I've done." I only said that to smooth things over—I didn't really mean it. I don't like to have to tell you that, but it's true. That's when we got back together and started having sex again.

I asked Dominique how he felt about sex, in light of his past experiences as an abuser and a victim of sexual abuse.

I felt if there were fewer boundaries when it came to sex, the better. Having lived in Europe, where sexuality and nudity are much more acceptable than they are here in the United States, I felt that was the way I wanted to live; with no boundaries and anything goes.

Dominique went back to talk about the sex he had with his sister:

The point is this: I knew it was wrong, but my mother didn't believe me and my father didn't seem to want to do anything about it, so I started to believe, at some point, that it was okay with him. I was still angry about my father's relationship with my sister. He was always protecting her. I felt that if I needed protection, no one was there for me.

Anger was a big part of it, even though I was sexually attracted to my sister. So much had happened, with my family, that I felt open, exposed—

and angry. I knew what I had done to my sister was wrong, but I wanted to get them back somehow. That was the reason why it still felt good in many ways.

The biggest part of it was sexual. I wanted it, and I did it.

At that point, I asked Dominique what he thought might have happened if his father had handled the situation differently and, perhaps, gotten him into therapy.

I believe that if he had addressed the situation and gotten me into therapy, it would have been less likely that I would have ended up here. I was sentenced to 20 years for my sexual crimes against my sister and my son—I'll tell you more about that later. I have served ten years so far, and I take full responsibility for all my actions. However, I believe in my heart that if my father had gotten me help when he found out what was going on; there's a chance I might not be here right now.

I told Dominique, that before we went on to the subject of his son, I wanted to give him the opportunity to say anything he thought might be helpful to people who might be thinking about molesting another person.

A few things come to mind. In school, when I joined the football team, my grades went from A's and B's to C's then D's as I transformed myself into the assault machine my coach wanted us all to be. I also felt that no matter what I did, God would always have my back.

I was big on isolation, too, as I've said, always spending lots of time alone in my room—which was painted black, by the way. I liked the darkness, and at some point I felt I needed it. Black walls, a TV, video games; I was using all those material things to try to make myself happy, but really, when I thought about it, was I happy? I don't think I was. I think it was just a need to succeed in escaping from reality for a little while.

I had also started drinking, back in Europe, and I smoked weed a few times too. Luckily, neither the liquor, nor the weed ever became a big problem. I just enjoyed it. It was another way I escaped from the real world and got away from all my problems.

Dominique went on to talk about the abuse that occurred to his son:

What happened between me and my son is hard for me to talk about. I went further with him than I did with my sister. When my mother told me she was going to treat her grandson the way she should have treated me, that felt good. It felt even better when she did it over the next few months.

My mother would tell him he was her favorite grandson, and then buy him anything he wanted. Whenever she did that, I couldn't help thinking, why hadn't she done that for me? It was then that I began to feel lots of resentment towards my son, a lot of jealousy. Even worse, there was no one I could talk to about the feelings I was having.

It didn't help that I felt like I was in a dead-end job again. It also felt like my relationship was going nowhere. When I asked myself what would make me feel better, at that point, I had trouble answering the question.

Meantime, I watched my son in the evenings because I worked the day shift, and my girlfriend worked nights. I didn't plan it, but one night when I was giving him a bath, I began to do the same things my cousin had done to me. I fondled him when I washed him, then afterwards while we were still undressed; I asked him if he wanted to wrestle.

I remember one night right before I laid down on top of him, he was on his stomach. He turned around and looked at me like he was afraid. That look made me so mad, I told him not to look at me. I told him that because I wanted to do what I wanted to do. I knew if he didn't stop staring at me, I wouldn't have been able to do it.

He did look away that night, and I did the same thing to him, I had done to my sister. When we finished, he got up and put his clothes on. No one ever found out what had happened, what I had done.

Things got worse after that, everything progressed. I got bored with the same routine, and I wanted to find new things to do and ways to justify what I was doing.

One of the things I did was blindfold my son, tying his hands behind his back, and taking pictures of him that way; an idea I had gotten from a movie I had watched when I was younger. That movie had portrayed an adult female being raped. My son was just six, at the time. After I took some pictures, I tried to penetrate him, but he jumped and I stopped. Afterwards, I untied him, removed the blindfold and helped him put his clothes back on.

I asked Dominique how he rationalized, or tried to rationalize, that behavior.

The things I did were triggered by anger and rage. I also had a hidden desire to tell someone they were going to get it, the desire to possess them, to say, "You're mine." At some point, I realized that came from my relationship with my mother.

My mother and I had all kinds of problems when I was growing up. One example was when I was 16 and a senior in high school. She told me I had to go get my picture taken, but I wanted to see my girlfriend, whom I knew was already pregnant. When my mother wouldn't let it go—or even let me out of the house, I pushed her, and she fell. One part of me felt sorry for pushing my own mother down, but another part wanted to say, "Hey, that's what you get!"

That kind of anger with my mother wasn't new to me either. I think it began in Europe, when she told me and my brother, she promised us really, that she was going to leave my father, but never followed through. When she did that, I got the message that she was choosing our father over us, and yes, it made me very, very angry.

Dominique went on to talk about how the fact that his father's mistress was also the choir director made everything even worse for him:

So here we were in church, singing about God loving us, and she was the one directing the choir. She was the one whose face I had to see each time as I sang. She was the same woman who was sleeping with my father. That really bothered me. It felt like such a huge betrayal!

That is why I tried to annoy her at practice. I would do little things like not stand up when she told us to stand up, and then sometimes, I deliberately sang in the wrong key. I think she suspected I knew what was going on between her and my father, but I don't think she knew for sure. Her son wanted to fight me once, for disrespecting his mother. I just looked at him and said, "You don't even know." Then I left.

Meanwhile, my mother had all these opportunities to leave my father, but she never took one of them. She chose my father over us, especially me. That's the way I saw it.

I asked Dominique if his course of treatment had helped his current relationship with his mother.

When I first got locked up back in '98, I could see my mother felt guilty about my imprisonment. She came to see me every weekend, and it was good at first. We talked, cried and laughed. I thought maybe since so much time had passed, we could have some sort of relationship.

We didn't stay close very for long. After I came here, she told me she thought my father was cheating on her again. I held her and told her I loved her. I don't know, maybe that bothered her. Whatever the reason, she never came back by herself. Looking back, I believe she might have told my father what she had told me. Maybe that was why she stopped coming to see me by herself.

Dominique went on to talk about his current contact with his family:

I see my family often, at least some of them. I had a big resentment against my father right around my 33rd birthday a few months ago. He had been putting the church ahead of me for a while and then decided not to visit me for my birthday. He went to take family pictures instead. I saw that as his way of trying to control me, something he had always done and something I had always resented.

Every year, my parents would send me a birthday gift in the amount of my age. So, that year the check was for $33.00. Enough is enough, is what I told myself before I sent the check back. My parents didn't like that—they took it personally and told me I had disrespected them by sending the check back.

A few weeks later, when my father and brother came up to see me, I knew I wanted to talk to my father and tell him how I was grownup, and I didn't want him trying to control me anymore. When I told him that, he turned it all around, blaming me for everything.

Then he said lots of things that bothered me. He told me I hadn't changed in the last ten years. Then he said *my* molestation never happened. He ended up by saying that if I wanted to be part of his family, I had to respect him. I asked him how I could respect him when, according to him. I hadn't changed at all in the last ten years. Then I said I didn't know whether we could have a relationship or not.

I know that hurt him, even though he's never been one to show it. Instead of telling me how he felt, he just sat there, and then told me that he could tell by my body language that I was frustrated.

That much was true! "Why can't you just connect with me? " I asked him. Clearly, that was not what he wanted to hear. He got up and walked out.

We haven't really had any relationship since then, even though I talked to him a few weeks later. I wanted to talk to my mother, too, to tell her it wasn't her fault. When she heard my voice and realized it was me on the phone, she hung up. When I called back, my father answered. When I asked him to tell my mother it wasn't her fault, he told me that to get to her, I would have to go through him.

He went on to tell me how he was sure I was telling everyone I didn't have a father, those days. I replied that I never denied he was my father, but I didn't know if I could go back to my family after my release, not when I felt that they were partially to blame for my problems.

My father reminded me that I needed a place to live. He also told me how my prosecutor had been in contact with him to make recommendations about the length of my prison term. I knew then that he was someone who felt he had to have power over me, even as an adult. That's why I gave him a message to give my mother, and then ended the call.

I didn't hear from either of my parents until right after Christmas when they sent me a Christmas card with the message: *You're never too old to be told what to do on the front* and: *And that's final* on the inside. I think my father picked it out, but both, he and my mother wrote on the card. The message I got was simple: *If you don't do what you're told, you're out in the cold, but God Bless.*

I went on to ask Dominique if he was up to telling me what had happened with his son. He replied that he was:

I took several pictures of my son in sexual positions, and then I stopped because I was afraid I'd get caught. I have often asked myself why I did that to my son. I think it all goes back to anger. The fact was I had become accustomed to pain from growing up in my family. If no one cared about me, then why should I care about my son? That was the reason I took those pictures and saved them, hiding them in a bedroom closet where I didn't think my girlfriend would ever find them.

One night, I felt like I just couldn't go on, couldn't do it anymore. I moved the pictures to the living room closet where I knew my girlfriend would probably find them. The next day, she went to work without leaving out any food for me. I checked the closet—the photos were gone. I called her job, but I knew she wouldn't be there. I knew she had gone to my parents' house.

It turned out that I was right about that. I was also right about the fact that after they saw the photos, my parents knew they had no choice but to call the police. The police came to get me about an hour later, and I told them everything. I confessed to everything.

Dominique was quiet for a few minutes, and I broke the silence by saying it sounded like he was ready to try to turn his life around, and I asked how he currently was doing.

I'm doing great. I feel like I've accomplished a lot here. I've reached Maintenance Level Five, at which point they say you've come to terms with what you've done and no longer need treatment. I've got a wonderful support team, as well as friends who actually care about me. I hold a couple of positions here, in the institution. I can do that because people here don't care about my past, they care about me.

I do a lot of opening up to people and sharing, talking about the things that really matter. I've learned a lot about myself being here. This is also the place where I grew up. I went from a boy to a man. None of it would have happened, unfortunately, if I had never been sent here.

I told Dominique that it sounded like the only thing he had ever really wanted to be was loved. I also reminded him that people who do bad things are not always necessarily bad people. I promised to relate his story accurately. I also thanked him for bringing my book full circle by being the voice who shared sexual abuse from a perpetrator's perspective. I believe his chapter will help my readers gain a deeper understanding of sexual abusers and their pain. Finally, I told him it had been an honor and a privilege to speak with him.

Dominique replied:

It's been an honor and a privilege for me, too. I had some doubts about doing this when I first heard about it. You know, I've just told you about my experiences here, about how I feel about everything I've done. I'm proud that I've shared my family experiences honestly with you, too, instead of reacting and acting out, something I always did, in the past.

There is Hope

There is always hope for tomorrow
through all the pain and sorrow.
From the fear, the helplessness, guilt and shame,
the anger, the sadness, the flashbacks, the pain.
Depression, anxiety, the low self-esteem,
the cold sweats, the sleepless nights, even the bad dreams.

My mind in turmoil trying to find a safe place to hide,
each day filled with guilt, so many nights I have cried.
Without a life raft, I drifted far out to sea,
calling for someone to come and rescue me.

The darkness had overshadowed me, there was no one in sight,
I raised my eyes upward, it was then I saw the light.
At that very moment, heaven's angels had appeared.
As the darkness had been lifted, my mind became very clear.

My hope was my confidence, a desire to start a new,
the hope of change to overcome all I have been through.
Hope was my boldness, after all my suffering and pain,
even with new found joy and peace,
my life will never be the same.

I will keep the hope alive each and every day.
For when God sent down His angels
I know it was He who paved the way.

Carol A. Ennis
© *2010*

Chapter Fifteen

Escaping The Shadows: Making the Shift from Survivor to Thriver — **Nickolas J. McDaniel**

"Be the change you wish to see in the world."
— *M. Gandhi*

"Freedom is a very expensive thing."
— *Rev. Dr. Martin Luther King, Jr.*

For just one moment, close your eyes and imagine opening them to a world that has just experienced an earthquake, the Big One. The landscape in front of you is both eerily familiar to the one you've always known, and yet, it is completely foreign at the same time. Your house and all of the buildings for as far as you can see are leveled; twisted piles of smoldering popped and snarled construction materials. People you know are wandering about bleeding, in a helpless, confused daze. Fear and anarchy now replace the social etiquette that you've always known and you're powerless to change, much less understand it. You can no longer trust the ground beneath your feet that has always been solid and dependable—aftershocks of varying magnitude can come at any time, day or night, and knock you down yet again…and again. Life as you know it will never, ever be the same.

Sexual abuse is like a large earthquake; a huge tectonic shift that rocks one's world and colors the lens through which the survivor views and interprets it. In the short term, an earthquake devastates; long-term, it forever alters the landscape. Likewise, in the short-term, sexual abuse devastates, and in the long-term, it alters the trajectory of the victim's life. In the documentary *Boyhood Shadows*[1], Glenn Kulik describes sexual abuse as being stabbed in the brain. Herbert Ward points out that abuse casts a shadow the length of a lifetime. I should know, as a child and an adolescent I experienced several incidents of violent sexual abuse from a male and several females. My life was forever changed...I was forever changed, never to be the same. The aftershocks of child abuse were devastating: drug use, an eating disorder, self-mutilation, morbid obesity, isolation, depression, sleep disturbances, difficulty concentrating in school...all just to name a few. By the time I was six years old, what I wanted to be when I grew up was—dead. By the time I was 19 years old I had dropped out of school and completely given up on living. No one expected me to see 30...and yet here I am knocking on the door of age 40, and living a happy and fulfilled life in a state of deep contentment, gratitude, acceptance and yes; self-love. It took a while, but I got there.

Others would describe me as outgoing, happy, and successful. I lost over 400 pounds, have a graduate degree, a respected professional and I'm living a life that I would describe as beyond my wildest dreams. So, how have people like myself made the transition from being an abuse victim controlled by aftershocks (the symptoms of Post-Traumatic Stress Disorder or PTSD) to become what is best described as a thriver?

In the course of my own healing, it was crucial to reclaim my voice. That was the most important thing. The very acts of sexual violence that had rocked my world and violated my body and sense of personal safety, had also effectively raped my voice from me. It had disappeared and my first step was to get it back. As such, in the process of healing it was integral to locate my voice for the very first time. It began with psych education: learning about one's sexual rights and assertiveness. These were tools I increasingly began to utilize in the course of my life. Soon

1   Rosen, S. & Teri DeBono (Producers). (2008). *Boyhood Shadows* [Documentary]. United States: Mac + Ava Productions.

it became apparent that speaking out on my own behalf was not enough; I had a deep desire to "give back." I realized how much stigma exists in regard to male survivors—being male and a victim is not acceptable. "Real men" are supposed to be the "strong, silent type" and "play through the pain" without shedding a tear. Sexual abuse is the ultimate vulnerability, the antithesis of the contemporary cultural definition of what it means to be a man in the United States. A male—no matter what the age—raped by women is impossible...yet this is what happened to me and sadly, I am not alone. Yet, these stereotypes exist, and the worst part of it is that there are impediments to male survivors getting the help they need to live productive lives. As such, I realized my story had the power to change the traditional definition of manhood, and make it easier for other survivors to come forward and seek help.

I began to speak. I speak for the innocent boy, I never got the chance to be. I speak for the other men who were wounded as boys by sexual violence. I spoke to audiences of all ages, genders, classes, ability levels, ethnic backgrounds, and educational levels. I began to appear in documentaries, articles, news stories...any medium to get the word out; to do what I could do to prevent for others, the devastating earthquake that had happened to me. I became addicted to education and advocacy as I had once been addicted to drugs and video games as a child and teen.

Yet that was not enough. I began to pursue a career as a helping mental health professional in a local Rape Crisis Center; a resource for male survivors struggling to come to grips with and rise above the destruction that abuse had caused. Finding my voice as an advocate, and standing up for others as no one had stood up for me as a child, was an empowering feeling. In the process, I not only found my voice and my calling, but I also realized I had the power to change this world for the better; to deeply touch audiences and invoke emotions such as sadness and triumph with my own voice as I told my story. I also realized I had the power to help other survivors, of all genders, to rise above what they had endured and become something more, something better. All precisely because they had experienced the devastation of childhood sexual abuse, just as I had.

Advocacy is an important tool in making the shift from survivor to thriver; not just for me, and not just for male survivors of childhood sexual abuse; but for anyone whose world has been rocked by trauma and has left them feeling powerless—voiceless. It can help survivors regain their voice and help them learn, for the first time, that they are powerful beings. More importantly, advocacy can rebuild a life formerly devastated by earth-shattering abuse. It can also forever alter a heart and soul and change it into something even more beautiful than it once would've been. Freedom from the shadows of childhood sexual abuse and the devastating aftershocks is possible. It can be both the hardest and best thing a survivor can do for himself or herself. I should know.

Chapter Sixteen

Breaking the Cycle of Sexual Abuse
— Stephen L. Braveman, M.A., L.M.F.T., D.S.T.

It seems that every time we turn on the television, listen to the radio, or open our web browsers, we are bombarded by stories of yet another priest, teacher or parent, sexually abusing a child. We are left wondering if sexual abuse of children is on the rise, or perhaps, is it that we simply hear more about it these days due to an increased awareness of the issue, and the overwhelming presence of data fed to us daily.

Regardless of the source, increased awareness of incidences of childhood sexual abuse has given rise to a huge increase in services being offered to assist those who have been wounded. Rape crisis centers are built, books are written and films are made. At the same time, ways to deal with the perpetrators have also grown at a tremendous rate. We keep passing new laws, building new prisons and creating new electronic tracking devices; all in an effort to control and contain the guilty. After all, who doesn't want to protect our innocent children and punish evil wrong-doers?

And yet, sexual abuse of children still continues!

Is there another answer? Another way we can really put a dent in, and, maybe, just maybe, stop childhood sexual abuse altogether?

This chapter explores basics elements that perpetuate sexual abuse of children. Particular attention is given to the role of early intervention, in our quest, for that ever elusive "ah-huh" moment that will allow us to be just as successful in ending sexual exploitation and abuse, as we are at putting humans into space, cracking the genetic code of our being, and creating the technology to accomplish such tasks.

Becoming Aware of Childhood Sexual Abuse

To break the cycle of sexual abuse we must first identify what exactly it is and recognize that it exists. This may be a task harder than one might think. Why? And haven't we known about this problem for a very long time? The answers to those questions are "yes" and "no" simultaneously.

Childhood sexual abuse is certainly not a new thing; it's simply a byproduct of modern times. Researchers have documented countless incidences around the world, in which humans have been known to molest children dating back to perhaps, the dawn of our species. This human pattern of abuse is clearly spelled out in *The Universality of Incest* (Lloyd DeMause, 1991). It gives examples of everything from "simple incest"—such as childhood marriage to adults—to elaborate rituals of mutalization for the purpose of sexualizing a particular body part, such as the Chinese tradition of "foot binding" with the purpose exaggerating the sexual quality of a women's foot, especially the large toe, are described in cultures all around the world. At the same time, we find numerous incidences of "innocent" rituals, in which, a culture has historically used sexual contact with children for a "noble" cause. *Gilbert Herdt*; Sambia Sexual Culture: Essays from the Field (Worlds of Desire: The Chicago Series on Sexuality, Gender, and Culture, 1999), describes how the *Semen Warriors of New Guinea*, a proud warrior tribe, ritually passed the strong warrior power of the adult males, onto the young warrior to-be boys, by way of having the boys swallow the semen of the adult warriors. It was a very special privilege to swallow semen from the biggest, strongest and bravest of them all.

As we take a close look at our universal past we find it is sometimes easy, sometimes hard, to define when sexual contact between children and adults constitutes abuse, and when it constitutes appropriate and, perhaps, "necessary" honored rituals. As our culture keeps evolving, so does our language and what we apply it to. We need to look at current, localized, American cultural norms, to define what is and isn't considered child sexual abuse today. We are lucky in that we now have a slew of great books, pamphlets, brochures, articles and films on this topic and, therefore; we do not need to recreate the wheel. In addition to this current text, two such books stand out from the crowd by describing childhood sexual abuse in a manner that adults can relate. Ellen Bass and Laura Davis's groundbreaking book, *The Courage to Heal: A Guide for Women Survivors of Child Sexual Abuse (1988)* set the tone. It was the first substantial book that both identified what sexual abuse looks like and, at the same time, offered a multitude of therapeutic strategies one can take to heal. Mike Lew's groundbreaking book on the sexual victimization of males, *Victims No Longer (1990)*, did the same. In addition, Lew's book opened the door to debunking the myth that males cannot be sexually abused; and lead many male victims toward healing. The original version of *Boyhood Shadows*: *I Swore I'd Never Tell*, made by The Monterey Rape Crisis Center and the MAC and *AVA Motion Picture Company (2008)*, helps viewers recognize the unique challenges male survivors of childhood sexual abuse face in a palatable, yet highly informative manner.

Chipping Away At The Cycle

Debunking myths about sexual abuse is now a therapeutic standard when it comes to self-help and professional treatment. It is also essential if we want to end sexual abuse. The more the victims learn about these myths, the less likely they are to be victimized again, and the less likely they are to go on and repeat the pattern.

One myth is that sexual abuse is always violent. Many are surprised to learn that sexual abuse includes non-physical incidences as well, such as being a witness to indecent exposure, receiving obscene phone calls or text messages, being the subject of voyeurism, being exposed to pornography, being a non-physically touched subject of pornography and living in an overly sexualized, emotionally incestual or sexually verbal inappropriate setting *(Laura Davis, 1991)*. In fact, according to the *T.A.S.K. (Take A Stand for Kids)* national website, kissing a child when they do not want to be kissed is considered to be a form of sexual abuse.

The image of what a sexual perpetrator looks like has been changing. Men have, and continue to be, the main culprit in most people's minds. The denial that a female could sexual offend has been very strong. We now recognize that, while at a lesser rate than males, females do commit sexual offenses despite the myth that they are not capable of doing so. Mothers, sisters, aunts and even grandmothers sometimes molest children *(Scott Abraham, 1997)* and at a rising rate *(Bureau of Justice Statistics, 2002)*. A fairly common occurrence is a female babysitter who explores a young boy's body while changing him and putting him to bed a night *(Mike Lew, 1990)*. Similarly, it is not uncommon for this author to hear female patients report that they were sexually abused by an older female under the guise of initiating the young girl into lesbian love.

Of course, just as with males who molest males, females who molest females are not doing this due to homosexual desire, but rather a desire for power and control over the victim.

Myths about Male Sexual Victimization" (Adapted from presentation at the 5th International Conference on Incest and Related Problems, Biel, Switzerland, August 14, 1991), describes dangerous, commonly held myths, specific to males who have been sexually abused as a child. These myths include such things as "the macho image" in which it is believed that boys cannot be sexually abused because they are strong. Of course, boys are children and are not capable of protecting themselves from adults any better than girls. This myth suggests that boys should just tough it out, or "man up", if they are abused. This means he should simply bury the issue and never receive help for it. The myth that only effeminate boys are sexually abused mixed with the myth that all males who sexually abuse boys are gay, plays havoc on the male victim's sense of self and his sexual orientation. If he grows up to be gay, then his orientation is supposedly caused by the abuse. Both are false in that very "macho" boys get abused at the same rate as not so macho boys. Extensive research has proven that same sex sexual abuse is not capable of causing one to become gay. Another strongly held myth is that boys cannot be sexually abused by females. The false notion that a boy must have an erection to have sex, and that he must want sex to have the erection, falsely leads people to believe that such boy-adult female contact must be consensual. Again, that train of thought is false and damaging in that it allows women to sexually abuse without consequences.

Perhaps the most damaging myth about sexual abuse of children is the one we call the "vampire syndrome", in which, like the victims of *Count Dracula,* once bitten, they will go on to bite others. It is clear to see how this myth is perpetuated. Research has clearly indicated that child victims of domestic violence are very likely to grow up and repeat the pattern if they do not receive help. Research also shows us that approximately 60 percent of career pedophiles were sexually abused themselves as a child. Abuse begets abuse. Logic puts these statistics together to form a perfect storm aimed at the demise of the sexually abused child. As a result of this myth, many sexual abuse survivors, both male and female, avoid working with children, avoid having children of their own, and sometimes avoid adult relationships all together; all out of unfounded fear that they might abuse the children in their lives. Similarly, many potential partners will call off a wedding or relationship ceremony out of fear that their partner, the survivor, will do such horrendous acts against their own children. However, the truth is far from this logical outcome. In reality, a very tiny percentage of those who have been sexually abused go on to abuse others. Even then, it is common that those who do repeat the crime are mentally ill, developmentally disabled, or still children at the time; meaning that they lack the mental capacity to really know what they are doing. The vast majority of victims/survivors would never abuse a child in this way because logic tells them how bad it was for them, and they vow to never repeat the pattern.

Healing The Couple: The Survivor And Their Partner

Just as the alcoholic is likely to relapse if their partner is not involved with treatment, the sexual abuse survivor's odds of acting out and, possibly, repeating the pattern of abuse, increase if their partner is not involved in the healing process. Survivors of sexual abuse typically find they cannot establish and maintain a healthy romantic, interpersonal relationship until they've completed significant individual and group psychotherapy. If they've been in a relationship, the relationship has most likely suffered tremendously. Healing for the couple comes through similar means as it did for the individual. Education and confrontation are essential. For example, it's important for both the survivor and the partner to recognize that the partner has now been victimized in the process of being in the relationship, not by the victim, but by the victimization of the victim. Together they have learned how pervasive the damage of sexual abuse can be. Together they can learn how to be partners in the healing.

The hand-out, *Outgrowing The Pain Together*, by Eliana Gil (1992), is especially useful when read, and discussed in detail, in helping couples coping with sexual abuse healing to understand what they need to do to heal. It addresses the 20 most common issues these couples face. The therapist can help the couple identify which, of any, of these 20 issues the couple still needs to face, and it helps develop much of the remaining treatment plan needed based upon the results. As the work progresses, classic and innovative "couple's methods of treatment" may be employed.

Early Intervention And Prevention

Two recent projects are breaking the cycle of abuse via early intervention methods. Both of these relatively new programs are showing promising results and may, in fact, be major contributors to ending sexual assaults.

The *Juvenile Sexual Offender Response Team (JSORT)* program, launched in Monterey, California in 2009, offers a new approach utilizing as many public service agencies and departments as possible when a youth is found to have committed a sexual offense. The concept is quite simple: intervene with a youth as soon as it is discovered that he or she has committed a sexual offense. If the child is young and relatively unaware, a "naïve perpetrator", they are provided with therapy and education. This combination is frequently sufficient to prevent further offenses. If the child is involved with a gang, therapy may occur within the context of group therapy and gang violence reduction programs. If the child is sentenced to time in the Youth Authority, therapy will occur within that setting. While these may sound like common place practices, they are actually innovative in that child sexual offenders have typically been dealt with similarly as adult offenders, resulting in punitive measures only—not treatment.

Another highly successful, relatively new kid on the block is the *My Strength Program*. This is a program geared toward keeping non-offending, male teens, from becoming offenders through education and positive group activities. Those who attend this program are given skills to use their own power to say, "No", when their sexual partner asks them "not to" and to say "No" when their sexual partner is not in a position to give permission, such as the case when their partner may be intoxicated. Group activities add to the program by providing peer relationships with those who are also taught to be powerful, by saying "No" to forcing unwanted sexual activity onto a partner.

When combined with other early childhood education programs, such as the *fun music* by Dr. Peter Alsop aimed at very young, to puberty-age children, teaching them how to stay "safe" from sexual violence; early intervention programs offer us hope. Perhaps the next generation of children will grow up with a zero tolerance for both being sexually abused, as well as, zero tolerance for becoming sexual offenders.

Conclusion

We are realistic. Those of us working in the field of sexual abuse treatment know that we will not see an end to sexual violence and abuse in our lifetimes. We have many who need healing and there is a lot of prevention work that still needs to be done. However, as we teach our children to recognize what sexual abuse is, how to stay safe, how to report sexual abuse if it does occur, and how to be strong and not offend, one day our long-time human pattern of existing with sexual abuse as part of our culture, may just perhaps come to an end.

Faith's Journey

Oh holy and everlasting spirit,
yes, I am still alive.
Because of my faith and your presence,
is the only way I could have survived.

I speak not of these words in silence,
of the mental and emotional pain,
but of how God showed me mercy
when He washed away the stain.

I ask where I would be today, if it wasn't for God's grace,
through all of my pain and suffering
I continued to seek His face.
In Him I have found peace and comfort,
He never left me alone.
He carried me when I had fallen
He helped me find my way home.

With God I have become a survivor,
I can now see through His eyes.
Each morning when I wake up,
I know it was Him who helped me to rise.

Carol A. Ennis
© *2010*

PART III

TAKING BACK YOUR POWER

Chapter Seventeen

Therapy as a Healing Journey
— Nan Wise, LCSW, ACSW, BCD

A number of years ago, Sharon asked me to write this chapter as she contemplated giving birth to this book. As a psychotherapist, and brain researcher, who has spent the past three decades teaching about emotional regulation and healing, I can think of nothing more joyful than sharing the insights and tools I have gathered along the way. Even though each healing journey is unique, as is each individual, there exists a rich collective of knowledge and wisdom that we can draw upon. I have been blessed with an abundance of brilliant teachers, compassionate therapists, wise mentors, and courageous clients; all of whom have taught me well. I thank you, Sharon, for this opportunity to pass on the wisdom of the collective. And to the reader, I say, you are not in this alone. You can draw upon the collective. We are all cheering you on. And as we take our individual healing journeys, we are making a huge contribution to the planet.

Lesson One: We are all unique, but at the same time, not.

We share more as human beings than what separates us. Experiencing something as devastating as sexual abuse tends to create a sense of isolation through shame and secrecy. Many people struggle with traumatic experiences of one sort or another. In fact, most people are recovering from some kind of wounding. And these hurts need not separate us, but unite us in the experience of being human. Everyone who has ever lived has experienced hurt and joy, pain and pleasure, hope and despair, shame and embarrassment, love and fear. And isn't it good to know that it is not what has happened to us that leaves the lasting wounds, but what we have been taught by those experiences about ourselves and the world. The negative beliefs about ourselves and the accompanying emotions of self-doubt, self-blame, fear, anger, helplessness, and difficulty trusting; all contribute to our feeling that we are *not* okay, and the world is *not* okay. These decisions we make, based on our past experiences, tend to run our automatic emotional habits and behaviors. As we release shame and secrecy, we can interact with self and the world based on present-time, conscious decisions, and deliberately alter the old beliefs and habits that no longer serve. We have awareness and choice. Choice sets us free to choose differently about how we see our past, our present, and our future.

Try on a new belief system: The past has happened, and although I can't change the events, I can change beliefs about myself and the world that arose from those experiences. I can choose to see myself as a survivor, rather than a victim of the past. And beyond surviving the past, I can choose to thrive in the present. And I can be loved and supported during the journey. No one heals alone!

Lesson Two: Listening to and loving the self, including the hurt parts of self we don't like or symptoms that plague us.

One of the most powerful lessons is to look for the positive intention underlying the symptom; and rather than trying to push the pain way, to embrace it. Leaning into the edges of what disturbs us, will allow unfinished emotional business to be addressed and integrated. Studies have shown that it is not the feelings themselves that cause long-term problems; but rather the withholding of the expression of the emotions connected with our experiences. It is through discharging our painful pasts that permits us to digest and absorb our experiences. And it is largely shame that inhibits people from sharing their distress because of the fears of social stigma that surround charged issues such as sexual abuse.

What we resist persists.

Here's my own story about shame and embarrassment.

I developed panic attacks as a young adult while working in a psychiatric hospital and I thought I was going crazy. I felt broken, and ashamed, as the anxiety threatened to derail me from being a "normal" person, attempting to embark on a career in psychology. What suffering ensued as I felt out of control of my body and my mind. How could I ever help anyone when I couldn't help myself? I hated those anxiety attacks, the feelings of unreality and the physical symptoms which plagued me. All I wanted was for them to go away forever.

The truth is that it was only after I started embracing my anxiety attacks rather than rejecting them that I started to heal. Once I befriended the panic attacks, shared openly with friends and colleagues about my affliction, and started to compare notes with others, that I realized that not only was I not alone, many people could relate to me, even if they had never experienced panic attacks before. It was an authentic me that began to emerge, as I listened deeply to what the anxiety was telling me: I was very anxious about life, I was trying too hard to be too perfect, I was pretty tough on myself in general. My love for self was conditional: I could love the in-control "clinical" me, but not the messy, anxiety ridden, vulnerable, emotional me. So, rather than seeing the panic attacks as a sign of pathology, I revamped my belief system to reflect them as gift to self. I was able to integrate all the aspects of my selves, and lose the fear of my fears. Not surprisingly, shortly thereafter, the panic attacks dissolved and I learned to practice a less conditional version of self-love that allowed me to be more real and authentic with others.

Another example: It is not uncommon for survivors of sexual abuse (or other forms of emotional pain) to self-medicate with drugs of abuse. Then the symptom of substance abuse becomes yet another reason to judge self and another symptom of the sexual abuse. What happens if you look at the positive intention of the part of the self that self-medicates?

What does that part really want? To hurt yourself more? Or something more positive?

If you dig deeper and assume a positive motivation for the behavior, even if ultimately that behavior doesn't help but hurt, my guess is you will probably find what that part wants is not to feel pain, not to hurt, but rather to feel some kind of control. What if you listened to that part of self and gave it a voice and a choice? Self-love is how people heal; not self-flagellation. We can consciously choose more positive behaviors if we listen lovingly to our symptoms.

Try on a new belief system: There is a positive intention underlying all symptoms and all behavior, even the stuff we don't want or understand.

Lesson Three: The most important conversation is the one happening between your ears.

Getting in touch with feelings of personal power is an important step in the healing process. One tool I use with clients is to teach them how to deliberately give themselves powerful, encouraging messages. We can suggest to ourselves very potent new beliefs that help us mobilize our healing powers. Hypnotherapy can be useful in making these deliberate, empowering suggestions to the self. This will counteract the negative messages we have learned that tend to be so automatic that we don't even notice them. We are always talking to ourselves, whether we are conscious of the internal dialogue or not. Becoming aware of the conversations going on between our own ears is crucial. Listen to how you speak to yourself, and you will learn a lot. Interrupt the negative messages you are inadvertently reinforcing, and you will begin to see that what you tell yourself is the most powerful medicine of all. Find a therapist who will help you steer yourself toward your conscious commitments and stay focused on what you want to create.

Try on a new belief system: I have all of the resources inside to help me find the external resources I need to thrive. I can make contact with my own powerfully resilient self and find all the assistance and support I need.

Lesson Four: We can learn to take our feelings as information, rather than facts. Listening to the body creates a pathway toward releasing old emotions.

Most emotions consist of sensations in the body, plus thoughts in the mind. We feel something in our body: perhaps a knot in the throat, or tightness in the chest, or tension in our muscles; and then create a label for those sensation-experiences. Very often, people who have experienced sexual abuse learn to protect themselves by shutting down the awareness of gut reactions that are expressed as sensations in the body.

Although such defenses were helpful at one time, they are now no longer needed now and actually become part of the problem by preventing the release and integration of old emotional experiences. *Gestalt therapy*, one particular approach to therapy that I find extremely helpful, encourages the individual to feel the sensations in the body that accompany being upset, and to stay with them until the feelings peak and release.

I once observed a woman who had been sexually abused as a young child by her stepfather confront old memories that were infused with powerful negative feelings. In a therapy session, she allowed herself to recall the incidents of abuse, and to feel all the sensations in her body associated with her experience of fear, rage, and confusion—and to stay present to those sensations. With a bit of coaching, she was able to allow the feelings to rise, peak, and release. She cried until she was done crying, and then she began to laugh—deep, resonating, belly laughs of joy and release. She experienced something very powerful: she could handle the feelings she had long attempted to avoid, and was indeed, a mature, capable adult.

Try on a new belief system: Whatever it is, I can handle it. I can feel sensations in my body and be aware of thoughts in my mind. I know that I am now capable of integrating my experiences and tolerating my emotions such that they will peak and release. I am getting lighter and more present to my joyous life with each passing day.

And finally, the most important lesson of all: We are self-healing creatures. Self-healing is the natural way. When we cut a finger, the body knows how to heal. When our psyches are hurt, the mind knows how to heal. And when our hearts are wounded, our hearts know how to find wholeness. We simply need to foster a nurturing, loving relationship with self (and others) to create the right context for the healing process.

And may you find great joy and love along the way!

Questionnaire

Denying the reality of abuse does not lessen its effect on the victim or on society. Not all the affects are as obvious as others, but they do exist. Once abused, the victim is never the same and because of behavioral changes, the effect of child sexual abuse begins affecting the child and the entire family immediately, generally in a negative way. At that point, a rippling affect begins, which impacts not only the child, but society as a whole due to actions of the victim. If they have no love for themselves, what will make them have love for their fellow man? It makes it easier for a victim to make unwise choices that can be disruptive and destructive to both, themselves and those around them. Imagine the impact that it has when measured against 39 million survivors.

I have developed a series of questions that have helped me to uncover the details of my trauma. Hopefully, they will help you to begin your healing process too. Please answer the questions as honestly as possible and be mindful about minimizing your experiences. These questions were created to help *you* to open up and motivate you to take back your power! No one has to see these answers but you. Please use additional paper to complete your answers if needed.

- At what age do you recall being sexually abused? Explain

- Please describe specific details of what you remember about the abuse?

- Who was your abuser and did you trust him/her?

- How did you feel after the abuse? Explain (example: ashamed, afraid, guilty, angry).

- Who did you tell after it happened? If you didn't, what kept you from telling anyone?

- How many times did the abuse happen?

- Did you block out the memories of the abuse and try to forget that it never happened?

- How did the abuse affect your behavior and how you interact with others? (example: drugs, prostitution, promiscuity, alcoholism, outbursts of anger, suicide).

- How would you say the abuse changed your life? (example: trust, intimacy, anger issues).

- Have you ever sexually abused someone or thought about doing it?

- Do you feel that the abuse has affected your ability to have healthy relationships with others?

- Has the abuse effected your self-esteem and given you a negative opinion about yourself?

- Are you ashamed of your body or being naked in front of others?

- Have you minimized the abuse or tried to convince yourself that it really wasn't that bad?

- Was your abuser(s) a family member?

- Have you ever considered therapy or counseling for the abuse? If not, are you willing to seek the assistance of outside help?

Resources for Help

Angel Wings Publications Website
http://www.angelwingspublications.com

ChildHelp
USA-National Child Abuse Hotline
Childhelp USA National Headquarters
15757 N. 78th Street
Scottsdale, Arizona 85260
1-800-4-A-Child / 1-800-422-4453
(TDD):1-800-2-A-Child / 1-800-222-4153
http://www.childhelpusa.org

Darkness to Light
http://www.darkness2light.org

Justice for Children
1155 Connecticut Avenue, N.W.
6th Floor
Washington, DC 20036
202.462.4688
http://www.jfcadvocacy.org

National Children's Alliance
516 C Street, NE
Washington, DC 20002
800.239.9950
http://www.nationalchildrensalliance.org

The National Crime Victim Bar Association
2000 M Street, N.W., Suite 480
Washington, DC 20036
800-FYI-CALL
202.467.8753
http://www.ncvc.org

New York State Domestic & Sexual Violence Hotline
800.942.6906

Rape, Abuse & Incest National Network
200 L Street, NW
Suite 406
Washington, DC 20036
202.544.3064
800.656.HOPE (800.656.4673)
http://www.rainn.org

Stop it Now!
351 Pleasant Street, Suite B-319
Northampton, MA 01060
Tel: 413.587.3500
Fax: 413.587.3505
 Helpline: 1.888.PREVENT
http://www.stopitnow.com

Survivors of Incest Anonymous (SIA)
P.O. Box 190
Benson, MD 21018-9998
410.893.33220
http://www.siawso.org

Recommended Books

Bass, E. and Davis, L. (2003) - *Beginning to Heal – A First Book for Men and Women Who Were Sexually Abused As Children* - New York: Collins

Brown, M.L. and Braveman, *S.L. – (2007) - CPR For Your Sex Life: How to Breathe Life Into a Dead, Dying or Dull Sex Life*- California: BookSurge, LLC

Jones, S. L. (2007) - *Enemy Between My Legs*- Redford, MI: Stephanie L. Jones, LLC

Williams, M.J. – (1991) *Healing Hidden Memories – Recovery for Adult Survivors of Childhood Abuse* - Deerfield Beach, FL: Health Communications, Inc.

Bowens, D. - (2007) *Hush Hush* - Yonkers, NY: ILERA, LLC

Bass, E. and Thornton, E. (Editors) - (1991) - *I Never Told Anyone – Writings by Women Survivors of Child Sexual Abuse*
New York: HarperPerennial

Blume, E.S. – (1993) *Secret Survivors- Uncovering Incest And Its After Effects In Women* New York: Ballantine Books

Bass, E. and Davis, L (1992) - *The Courage to Heal - A Guide for Women Survivors of Sexual Abuse* - New York: Harper Collins

Spirituality and Encouragement:

Coehlo, P. - *(2006) - The Alchemist –*New York*:* HarperCollins

Taylor, S.L. (1994) - *In the Spirit* - New York: HarperPerennial

Ruiz, D.M. – (1997) - *The Four Agreements* - California: Amber-Allen Publishing

Vanzant, I. – (1996) – *Faith In The Valley* - New York: FIRESIDE

References

Arrien, A. (1991), Lessons From Geese, Transcribed from a speech at the Organizational Development Network and based upon the work of Milton Olson.

Bass, E, & Davis, L. (1994), The Courage to Heal: A Guide for Women Survivors of Child Sexual Abuse (third Edition), New York, HarperCollins.

Davis, L. (1991), Healing: When the Person You Love Was Sexually Abused As a Child. New York, HarperCollins.

DeMause, Lloyd (1991), The Universality of Incest, The Journal of Psychohistory, Fall 1991, Vol. 19, No. 2

Gartner. R. B., (1999), Betrayed as Boys: Psychodynamic Treatment of Sexually Abused Men, New York, The Guilford Press.

Gil, E. (1992), Outgrowing The Pain Together, New York, Dell Publishing.

Herdt, Gilbert, Sambia Sexual Culture: Essays from the Field (Worlds of Desire: The Chicago Series on Sexuality, Gender, and Culture), 1999, the University of Chicago Press, Chicago, Illinois.

Hunter, M. (1990), Abused Boys the Neglected Victims of Sexual Abuse, New York: Fawcett, Columbia.

Hunter, M. (1990), The Sexually Abused Male – Vol. 1, Prevalence, Impact and Treatment, New York, Lexington Books.

Hunter, M. (1990), The Sexually Abused Male – Vol. 2, Application of Treatment Strategies, New York, Lexington Books. 5th International Conference on Incest and Related Problems, Biel, Switzerland, (1991)

"Myths about Male Sexual Victimization" (Adapted from presentation), Geffner, R. (2003), Journal of Child Sexual Abuse, Canada, The Haworth Maltreatment & Trauma Press.

Lew, M. (1990), Victims No Longer, New York, Harper Collins.

Steen, C. (2001), The Adult Relapse Prevention Workbook, Brandon, VT, Safer Society Press.

The Monterey County Rape Crisis Center (2008), Boyhood Shadows: I Swore I'd Never Tell, original release version, the MAC and AVA Motion Picture Company, Monterey, California.

BIOGRAPHIES

Stephen L. Braveman, M.A., L.M.F.T., D.S.T.

Stephen L. Braveman, M.A., L.M.F.T., D.S.T., is a Licensed Marriage & Family Therapist (#MFC 28926), AASECT (American Association of Sexuality Educators, Counselors and Therapists) Certified Diplomat of Sex Therapy, AASECT Certified Supervisor and Certified CE Provider, Gender Specialist, Member of The World Professional Association for Transgender Health and Tantra/Sacred Sexuality Facilitator-Practitioner. Stephen currently serves as the Professional Sex Therapy Certification Committee Chair for AASECT and has served as the SSSS (The Society for the Scientific Study of Sexuality). Western Region 2009 Conference Co-Chair. He is a Past President and current Board of Directors member of MC-CAMFT (Monterey County Chapter of the California Association of Marriage and Family Therapists). He has served on the Board of TASK (Take A Stand For Kids), is an awarded member of Male Survivor for his leadership in treating Male Survivors of Sexual Abuse and Assault, for which he co-chaired the first National Retreat for Male Survivors of Sexual Abuse.

Stephen is the author of *Innovative Methods of Treating Patients with Sexual Trauma, Innovations in Clinical Practice: Focus on Sexual Health,* and CPR *for Your Sex Life: How to Breathe Life Into a Dead, Dying or Dull Sex Life which is* Co-Authored by Mildred Brown, Ph.D. He has a full-time Private Practice in Monterey, California. He has over 32 years of experience treating a wide variety of psychological and sexual disorders and issues. People seeking professional sex therapy in Monterey, California, professional transgender care in Monterey, California, professional sex therapy in Santa Cruz, California or professional transgender care in Santa Cruz, California have been able to turn to Stephen for these services since 1992. Stephen currently specializes in treating sexual disorders (while working just as much with women, he is best known for his innovative methods and projects working with male survivors of sexual abuse and/or rape - see extensive articles and links on this site), working with gender and transgender issues (see the article "What IS A GENDER SPECIALIST" on this site), bringing Sacred Sexuality/Tantra into the clinical hour and supervision. He is also a Consultant for the Human Rights Campaign's *"Coming Out - Transgendered"* brochure. Stephen supervises both Marriage and Family Interns and Sex Therapy Interns in Private Practice (currently, Carmen Martin, Registered MFT Intern) and Nickolas McDaniel, MFT Intern (also at the Monterey Rape Crisis Center) and others for AASECT Certification via their own private practice or agency.

He is a regular contributing author for the *IFriends* Love and Health website. Stephen's work has also appeared in many professional publications; such as *Rolling Stone Magazine, US News Magazine, Men's Health Magazine, Treating Abuse Today, The Monterey County Herald, The Monterey County Coast Weekly, The California Therapist, the AASECT Contemporary Sexuality* and a multitude of newsletters for various organizations. Stephen has taught Graduate Psychology classes (such as the *Assessment and Treatment of Sexual Disorders, Abnormal Psychology and Research Methods*) at both Chapman University and City University, and Undergraduate Psychology classes (such as *Human*

Sexuality and Psychology of Human Relations) at both Hartnell College and Vista College.

Stephen is a frequent workshop and conference presenter. He has provided in-service trainings, lectures and workshops for groups and associations such as AASECT Annual Conferences, SSSS Annual Conferences, The California Dreamin' Annual Transgender Conferences, The California Association of Marriage and Family Therapists, the Santa Cruz Family Services Agency, the Women's Crisis Center of Salinas, The Esalen Institute, The Monterey County Rape Crisis Center, PFLAG, Catholic Charities, The Beacon House, TASK (Take A Stand For Kids), the Monterey Medical Association and at many schools and university. He is frequently seen on TV (e.g. KSBW, KION) and heard on radio (e.g. Playboy Radio) and internet pod casts, as a spokesman for various projects and an expert on sexual issues.

Nickolas J. McDaniel

An inspirational speaker, advocate and compelling writer; Nickolas J. McDaniel has spoken to audiences across the United States and appeared in documentaries and publications regarding gender variance and male sexual abuse. In addition, Nickolas is also teaching college and seeing clients as a psychotherapy intern, sex therapy intern, and gender specialist intern through the Monterey County Rape Crisis Center and also through private practice.

Nan Wise, LCSW, ACSW, BCD
Creator of The Desire Curve

Licensed Psychotherapist

Nan Wise has twenty-five years of experience in individual, group, marital and family therapy.

She is:

Certified Sex Therapist, AASECT
- Fellow, The American Psychotherapy Association,
- Certified Relationship Specialist
- Board Certified Clinical Hypnotherapist
- Board Certified Diplomat of the American Board of Examiners in Clinical Social Work
- Doctoral Fellow in Cognitive Neuroscience, Rutgers University

In addition to her practice with mainstream couples and singles, Ms. Wise has spent the past decade providing relationship coaching and psychotherapy for individuals and couples practicing alternative lifestyles. More open, tolerant and accepting than most therapists, she says: "My primary goal in therapy and coaching is to get people to recognize and challenge their assumptions and then make choices that empower them and create good outcomes for themselves and in their relationships."

She observed that some of her non-monogamous clients were able to handle the ebb and flow of desire in their relationships as well as jealousy issues. What she learned from them helped her create the Desire Curve.

Ms. Wise has been trained in numerous therapeutic modalities including:

- Cognitive-Behavioral Therapy
- Gestalt Psychotherapy
- Eriksonian Hypnotherapy
- Psychodynamic Psychotherapy
- Neurolinguistic Programming (NLP)

Additionally, she was trained in meditation and behavioral medicine at Harvard Medical School's Mind/Body Institute, is a yoga teacher and certified Radical Honesty trainer.

Her therapeutic approach blends these modalities, disciplines and skills to create a dynamic and unique way of helping clients learn Operational Intelligence, a phrase she coined to describe learning how to operate emotional sexual systems. "It is a big step beyond emotional intelligence," she says.

Neuroscience Co-investigator
Her first post-graduate work at Rutgers University was in the field of neuroscience which she says is her "first love." While earning an M.S.W. in Social Work, she continued to read and study independently in neuroscience, a discipline which heavily influences her work, especially the creation of the Desire Curve. Then in 2007 she was invited by Dr. Barry Komisaruk and Dr. Beverly Whipple (co-authors of *The Science of Orgasm*) to be a co-investigator on their prestigious fMRI brain scan studies on orgasm and pain. She is currently a doctoral fellow in cognitive neuroscience at Rutgers University.

"My goal now is to pursue neuroscience studies and research more actively," she says. "I feel like I have come to the place I want to be where I can use what I am learning in neuroscience to help clients, students, the people who take my workshops—and readers of my articles."

Teacher, Speaker and Workshop Leader

- Ms. Wise is currently teaching a graduate course in Clinical Sexology for marriage and family therapists at Seton Hall University where she is an adjunct professor.

- Ms. Wise is a lecturer in psychology at Rutgers University, currently teaching classes on the Psychology of Relationship.

- A member of AASECT (American Association of Sex Educators, Counselors and Therapists), she conducted two workshops at the annual conference in 2006. (Presenters at AASECT conferences are leaders in their field; and attendance at the workshops count as credit toward certification.) Her workshops: Polyamory and Other Forms of Negotiated Non-Monogamy: A Crash Course for the Curious and Beyond Monogamy: Varieties of Loving and Committing. At the 2008 conference, she will present a workshop on Operational Intelligence.

- In part as the author of a series of articles on relationship healing for *Loving More* Magazine, Nan Wise was propelled into speaking engagements as a nationally recognized expert on new paradigm relationships. She is a frequent presenter, keynote speaker and workshop leader at Loving More Conferences, The Institute for Twenty First Century Relationships, The Midwest Alternative Polyamory Conference, among others.

Media Appearances, the Highlights

- An episode of *The Tyra Banks Show* that aired initially on October 9, 2006.

- An episode of *The Montel Williams Show* devoted to polyamory. November, 2005.

- "Family Values," an episode of Penn & Teller's Emmy-nominated Showtime series, *Bullshit!* May, 2005.

- *Loving & Cheating*, a Sugar Pictures documentary by Thom Powers (*Breasts; Private Dicks: Men Exposed*). February, 2005.

- "Beyond Monogamy," an episode of *The Sex Files*, the number-one-rated show on the Discovery Channel in Canada. Fall 2004

- "Scenes from a (Group) Marriage," a 1999 feature story in *Esquire* magazine. The article ignited Hollywood's interest with offers from Michael Douglas and Cameron Crowe.

- "Four in a Bed", an article appearing in *Eve* magazine, a U. K. publication for women, and reprinted in Australian *Marie Claire*, 2004.

- Domestic and international radio interviews for programs including *The Jay Thomas Show* on Sirius Radio, *The Maurice Boland Show* on Radio Europe Mediterraneo, and the BBC's *The World Today*.

- "Expert" quoted in The New York Post, The London Observer, the Chicago Sun-Times, and the Baltimore Sun, among other publications.

- *"Try My Life"* the Style network's reality show in which she exchanged lives with her daughter Julia for a day.

- The number-one-rated show on the Discovery Channel in Canada. Fall 2004

- "Scenes from a (Group) Marriage," a 1999 feature story in *Esquire* magazine. The article ignited Hollywood's interest with offers from Michael Douglas and Cameron Crowe.

- "Four in a Bed", an article appearing in *Eve* magazine, a U. K. publication for women, and reprinted in Australian *Marie Claire*, 2004.

- Domestic and international radio interviews for programs including *The Jay Thomas Show* on Sirius Radio, *The Maurice Boland Show* on Radio Europe Mediterraneo, and the BBC's *The World Today*.

- "Expert" quoted in *The New York Post, The London Observer,* the *Chicago Sun-Times*, and the *Baltimore Sun,* among other publications.

- *"Try My Life"* the Style network's reality show in which she exchanged lives with her daughter Julia for a day.

About the Author

Sharon R. Wells

Without Permission is a powerful and inspirational contribution to self-help literature on sexual abuse and spirituality.

Sharon R. Wells is a native of Philadelphia, Pennsylvania, a writer, radio show host, entrepreneur and motivational speaker. Using her own personal testimony of survival for illustration, she is a passionate advocate who speaks towards awareness and prevention of sexual and domestic abuse. With a message focused and centered on encouraging hope, unwavering faith and perseverance, Sharon guides others to realize, evaluate and triumphantly overcome the obstacles in their own lives through self-awareness and individual growth. This author of several articles and essays has written heartfelt, spiritual and inspirational messages highlighting her own individual healing journey while encouraging and uplifting others to do the same in their life. Having been a molestation victim herself, Sharon has been driven to raise awareness about the sexual abuse epidemic that exists in our society. Astoundingly, she has risen above her adversities, and her heroic courage will empower you to take the path to a new beginning in reclaiming your right to a healthy and happy life.

She is a beacon of light and her story will take you to that secret place in her life where she shares her own personal experiences of battling a history of alcoholism, drug addiction, unhealthy relationships, severe depression and self-hatred.

Sharon also is the founder and CEO of Angel Wings Publications, LLC, a corporation which provides resource information for sexual abuse victims and those that have been affected by it.